The

CHAPTER 1
MAN'S PERSPECTIVE

The Bible clearly says that God's thoughts are not our thoughts neither are His ways our ways and yet, man continually starts with his own perspective or interpretation and then interprets God's word based on this perspective. A good example of this is the darkness we see in the universe when we look up at the night sky. From man's perspective, it appears that the universe is endless darkness with the exception of the galaxies and stars that provide a little break-up of what is otherwise 95% darkness.

They then take this man-made perspective and apply it to God's word to form opinions and come to conclusions. The Creation account is a very good example of this. Based on man's perspective, we live in an eternity of darkness. So God necessarily had to fix this by creating light. The Bible confirms this in the creation account in Genesis 1:3.

Genesis 1:3 KJV

3 And God said, Let there be light: and there was light.

So now we have biblical confirmation of our own perception. A universe of eternal darkness needs light, so God created light; or did He?

Man will always run into problems when he makes decisions on what God's word means or is saying based on the limited perspective and observations we have. As Christians, we know God's word is the ultimate authority on truth. Does that mean we don't need observation or scientific analysis? In short, no. There isn't anything wrong with comparing the scientific data with what God's word says. However, a lot of what man calls science is just opinion or conjecture. Evolution is a perfect example of this.

It is critical to start with God's word alone and then we observe and form our perspective based on what the word of God says. The same thing applies to science. After all, real science is the study of creation.

Hebrews 11:3 KJV

Through faith we understand that the worlds were framed by the word of God, so that

things which are seen were not made of things which do appear.

As Christians, we know the word of God is what formed all creation. Hebrews 11:3 is not the only biblical text that confirms this fact.

John 1:1-3 KJV

1 *In the beginning was the Word, and the Word was with God, and the Word was God.*

2 *The same was in the beginning with God.*

3 *All things were made by him; and without him was not any thing made that was made.*

When science lines up with God's word, we can know that they have reached the correct conclusion.

At this time I want to point something out. The "Word" mentioned in John 1:1 is making reference to Jesus Christ.

There is profound and amazing biblical understanding that will come when we realize that the "Word" is Jesus Christ and also the information in the biblical text at the same time.

This does not make much sense when looking at it from man's perspective, but we have to remember what God's word says, and then abide by those rules when forming our conclusions.

Isaiah 55:8 KJV

8 *For my thoughts are not your thoughts, neither are your ways my ways, saith the Lord.*

In a manner of speaking, this takes a small step of faith. We need to forget the conclusions we would come to based on our perspective. We need to first apply what God's word says and then look around and see how God's word applies to, and confirms, what we perceive.

If God's word does not confirm our perspective, we need to re-evaluate our perspective.

Why?

Because God's word is truth and our perspective is very limited for several reasons, many of which will get covered in this book.

Look at it this way: truth does not conform to our perspective.

Truth is not flexible. It is the same, regardless of how we may perceive things in our world, universe, and reality.

Keeping that in mind, I want you to consider a biblical fact. The word of God is truth.

Truth never changes. Jesus is the Word. Jesus never changes.

Hebrews 13:8 KJV

Jesus Christ the same yesterday, and today, and for ever.

I am laying these foundational Christian truths out for you now because they are facts and they have profound and amazing implications that you will discover later on in this book.

Later in this book when I make statements that confirm the easy-to-understand plain-text facts of the Bible, such as: Jesus is the Word – or - Jesus and/or the Word are 100% truth.

Remember, truth never changes.

Do not question the biblical facts that I am stating, but instead question your perception. Remember what we went over: God's word comes first. Man's perspective needs to be based on God's word and not the other way around.

We confirmed that Jesus Christ is the same forever, but if He is literally God's Word, then God's Word should also be the same - never changing and lasting forever.

Matthew 24:35 KJV

Heaven and earth shall pass away, but my words shall not pass away.

Now let's get back to a universe that seems to be eternal darkness from man's perspective. It is a fact that this is man's observation from man's perspective. No one can argue against that point. Beyond the stars, the darkness seems to extend forever.

Now we will start with some amazing and profound truths. Man has incorrectly based the creation account on this perspective.

They started with the way man perceives things in our universe and reality and then interpreted God's word based on man's perception rather than start with what God's word actually says, and then interpreting what we perceive based on the word of God.

We will get back to the creation account in very fine detail, but before we do let's see what God's word actually says pertaining to the idea that eternity could be filled with darkness.

It is a biblical fact that heaven and earth will pass away.

I wrote this book with the guidance of the Holy Spirit and Bible believing Christians are my targeted audience. The Bible is fact and will always trump man's perception. With that in mind, let's see what the Bible says regarding eternal darkness or light.

According to the Bible, there is only one entity that has always been and will always be.

Revelation 1:8 KJV

I am Alpha and Omega, the beginning and the ending, saith the Lord, which is, and which was, and which is to come, the Almighty.

It is, therefore, biblical fact that only God has always been and will always be. God is the biblical definition of eternity. So, pertaining to eternal light or eternal darkness, what does the Bible say?

1 John 1:5 KJV

This then is the message which we have heard of him, and declare unto you, that God is light, and in him is no darkness at all.

Forget man's perception and consider what you just read. God is light and God is eternal.

There isn't any darkness in Him at all. It is a biblical fact that eternity is lit by God's light or Glory.

Psalm 8:1 KJV

To the chief Musician upon Gittith, A Psalm of David. O LORD our Lord, how excellent is thy name in all the earth! who hast set thy glory above the heavens.

Psalm 113:4 KJV

The LORD is high above all nations, and his glory above the heavens.

Consider this: Our universe is made up of about 95% darkness. Because of this many people assume darkness is the default position. For example, we turn off the lights and what do we have? Obviously - darkness.

However, darkness is not the default. Darkness is in fact just the absence of light. Einstein could see this;

"Darkness does not exist either. Darkness is, in reality, the absence of light.

Light we can study, but not darkness. In fact, we can use Newton's prism to break white light into many colors and study the various wavelengths of each color.

You cannot measure darkness. A simple ray of light can break into a world of darkness and illuminate it. How can you know how dark a certain space is? You measure the amount of light present. Isn't this correct? Darkness is a term used by man to describe what happens when there is no light present."

So, the real question is: Why is our universe in 95% darkness? Darkness, in the Bible, is connected to God's judgement, curses, a lack of understanding of God's Truth/Word, and separation from the Lord.

The ultimate example of this is given in Matthew 8:12 when God cast those who are of the kingdom of Satan into outer darkness.

Matthew 8:12 KJV

But the children of the kingdom shall be cast out into outer darkness: there shall be weeping and gnashing of teeth.

This explains why our universe is 95% darkness. God put our universe under a veil of darkness after the fall of Satan.

Isaiah 50:3 KJV

"I clothe the heavens with blackness, and I make sackcloth their covering."

Eternity beyond this veil is lit by God's glory.

The Bible makes a lot of factual statements in the plain text that most people dismiss as metaphorical.

I started noticing this a few years ago.

It happens over and over again, and it lines out perfectly with the science of quantum physics down to the finest details.

This happens far too often to ever be able to explain it away as random chance occurrences. You will notice this over and over again throughout this book.

Here is an example of a Bible verse that is saying eternity is lit by God's glory:

Psalm 113:4 KJV

The LORD is high above all nations, and his glory above the heavens.

The 'heavens" mentioned here is our universe of 95% darkness. Everything beyond our universe is lit by God's glory.Remember, this is just one verse among many.

So, we can see how a creation, starting with total darkness, makes sense from man's perspective but does not line up with the word of God.

When man places God and His word in a proverbial box, based on man's limited perspective, he misses out on most of the "bigger picture" that is demonstrated in the Bible.

God's thoughts and ways far exceed man's as does the depth of understanding that is written in His word. Let's take another look at Isaiah 55:8-9:

Isaiah 55:8-9 KJV

> **8** *For my thoughts are not your thoughts, neither are your ways my ways, saith the LORD.*

> **9** *For as the heavens are higher than the earth, so are my ways higher than your ways, and my thoughts than your thoughts.*

Now let's take a look at what the Bible says about the word of God.

Hebrews 4:12 NLT

> *For the word of God is alive and powerful.*

It is sharper than the sharpest two-edged sword, cutting between soul and spirit,

between joint and marrow. It exposes our innermost thoughts and desires.

With those verses in mind, you will see, as you get deeper into this book, that the Bible has several layers of deep understanding that is still kept within the correct biblical context.

Hebrews 4:12 is another example of a verse that most think of as metaphorical when it mentions the word of God as "living".

One of the amazing facts that you will discover in this book is that Hebrews 4:12 literally means that God's word is alive.

I would have never been able to come to these conclusions without deep investigation after taking the Bible literally.

We can only get the correct results in God's word when we follow the plain-text rules that we find in the Bible.

Does faith come first by observation? Take the darkness in the universe for example. Do we then interpret God's word based on this observation?

No!

Romans 10:17

Faith comes through hearing, and hearing by the word of God.

Since we know that God is light and yet the creation account seems to indicate that our universe started in darkness, we can also know that when God said; *"let there be light",* light entered our universe from eternity, or if you want the scientific definition, from another dimension.

The Bible says that God made man in His image. This is a strong indication that man is the apex of creation in our universe.

However, within God's word is deep wisdom and knowledge.

What do I mean by that? To be made in God's image not only gives us a clue to our physical location in the universe, but it also gives more depth to other scripture when used in the correct context.

If Christ dwells in us then we should reflect His image, spiritually speaking.

James 1:23-25 (ESV)

23 For if anyone is a hearer of the word and

not a doer, he is like a man who looks intently at his natural face in a mirror.

24 *For he looks at himself and goes away and at once forgets what he was like.*

25 *But the one who looks into the perfect law, the law of liberty, and perseveres, being no hearer who forgets but a doer who acts, he will be blessed in his doing.*

There are several layers of scripture just in these three verses.

1st Layer: It is saying that our lives, or actions, should reflect Jesus who lives inside us.

2nd Layer: It describes this mirror as the perfect law which is giving us a deeper understanding of Jesus Christ. This will be explained in depth later on.

3rd Layer: It is giving us an idea of our place in the universe. We were created in God's image.

The most amazing part about all three layers is that they are not speaking figuratively, but literally! This fact will also be proven in later chapters.

This would indicate that our neck of the woods is truly at the center of the universe.

First, let's see if we can find anything in God's word that would confirm this.

Remember, the truth is reached by starting with God's word and then verifying our finding through observation and science.

If we can pinpoint our location in the universe we should be able to locate a dimensional portal that would be a large projection of light, or what science would call the theoretical white-hole, that occurred when God said; *"let there be light."*

The Bible gives us two reference points that we can use to pinpoint our location. Both reference points are "water".

The Bible says that the boundaries of our universe above the heavenly firmament (where the sun, moon, and stars are located) are made of water.

The very next reference point that the Bible gives is the water on the earth. It literally says that God divided these waters that surround our universe from the waters on earth in the creation account of our universe.

Let's take a look:

Genesis 1:6-10 KJV

6 *And God said, Let there be a firmament in the midst of the waters, and let it divide the waters from the waters.*

7 *And God made the firmament, and divided the waters which were under the firmament from the waters which were above the firmament: and it was so.*

8 *And God called the firmament Heaven. And the evening and the morning were the second day.*

9 *And God said, Let the waters under the heaven be gathered together unto one place, and let the dry land appear: and it was so.*

10 *And God called the dry land Earth; and the gathering together of the waters called he Seas: and God saw that it was good.*

So, we know that the waters under the heaven are the seas of the earth. People have mistakenly assumed that the waters above the heavens are the clouds. But this is another example of man translating God's word based first on man's perspective.

We know that earth's rain clouds are not

located up with the sun, moon, and stars that the Bible clearly says are in the upper firmament. This is verified in verses 14-17.

Genesis 1:14-17 KJV

14 *And God said, Let there be lights in the firmament of the heaven to divide the day from the night; and let them be for signs, and for seasons, and for days, and years:*

15 *And let them be for lights in the firmament of the heaven to give light upon the earth: and it was so.*

16 *And God made two great lights; the greater light to rule the day, and the lesser light to rule the night: he made the stars also.*

17 *And God set them in the firmament of the heaven to give light upon the earth,*

We have biblical verification that the sun, moon, and stars are located in the firmament of the heaven. Remember, the upper waters are described as being "above" the firmament of the heavens. Let's take another look.

Genesis 1:6-8 KJV

6 *And God said, Let there be a firmament in the midst of the waters, and let it divide the waters from the waters.*

7 *And God made the firmament, and divided the waters which were under the firmament from the waters which were above the firmament: and it was so.*

8 *And God called the firmament Heaven. And the evening and the morning were the second day.*

We see that the stars exist in the upper firmament and that the waters are above this firmament.

These waters surround - or frame - our universe.

The only other reference point is earth. If this analysis, based on God's word first, is correct, then the earth would be at the center of the universe because the waters on earth are the only other focal point given.

I will bring the scientific verification into this later in this book, but before I do I want to point out some very interesting things the Bible seems to say if we are taking its descriptions literally.

The Bible says that God spoke the universe into existence.

To speak, meaning He used words when he said; *"let there be light."*

Hebrews 11:3 seems to point to the exact location the creation account gives for the waters that surround or frame our universe.

Hebrews 11:3 KJV

> **3** *Through faith we understand that the worlds were framed by the word of God, so that things which are seen were not made of things which do appear.*

If the worlds are framed by God's word, as Hebrews clearly says, and we take the creation account literally, His word would be a vast amount of water. Now, this really doesn't make any sense.

But that's looking at things from man's perspective.

It is not by chance that the Bible literally says God's voice sounds like a vast amount of water.

Ezekiel 43:2 KJV

> *And, behold, the glory of the God of Israel came from the way of the east: and his voice was like a noise of many waters: and the earth shined with his glory.*

> **Revelation 14:2 KJV** *And I heard a voice from heaven, as the voice of many waters.*

People will claim I am taking scripture out of context because I am taking it too literally.

I want to put this to rest now, at the beginning of this book.

After all, this book is called *"The Gap Fact"*. This means that I will prove the creation account by taking what the Bible says as literal and then checking to see if history and science confirm God's literal word.

So, let's walk by faith and not by sight, or by man's limited perspective, and see what we actually observe.

Remember, a real scientific discovery should include observable evidence. We can make observations through any one of the five senses that God has given us. In this situation, we will need to use our hearing to verify that God's voice literally sounds like a vast amount of water and this water literally frames our universe.

So, let's go to the exact location given by literal scripture and see what we find.

Before we go to the scriptural location, let's listen to what a vast amount of water sounds like so that there will be no mistaking it when we hear it in the biblical location given in His word. Any large amount of flowing water will do, but a perfect example, in my opinion, would be Niagara Falls.

If you have a computer nearby, please go to YouTube and type in "10 hours of Niagara Falls at Night". This will let you know exactly what you should hear when we go to the literal biblical location.

Now forget what man says and just trust the word of God - literally.

Let's go to the edge of the universe, or the cosmic background, and take a listen. Go back to YouTube and type in "Cosmic Background Radiation Ambient Noise".

Be honest with yourself. Did you just hear a vast amount of flowing water in the distance of space?

This is what we call observable scientific verification that we arrived at by taking God's word literally. Sure, you can say it's just several amazing coincidences that defy all odds.

I would say this is because you are placing man's observations and what you have been taught and told above what God's word literally says.

Later on in this book I will give the scientific verification for what you just heard, and it's exactly what your ears told you it was: a vast amount of water that God used to frame and form our universe/reality.

For those of you who may still be doubting the observation that you just made with your ears, hopefully, you will believe another observation that you can make to confirm these findings using your eyes.

This will be an observation of deep space to confirm that water does in fact "frame" our universe.

I would like to show you the results of the Millennium Run project.

The Millenium Run used more than 10 billion particles to trace the evolution of the matter distribution in a cubic region of the Universe over 2 billion light-years on a side.

It kept busy the principal supercomputer at the Max Planck Society's Supercomputing Centre in Garching, Germany for more than a month.

This is a photo of their results that is placed directly below water.

Upon viewing these photos you will have verified the biblical findings with both your hearing and sight.

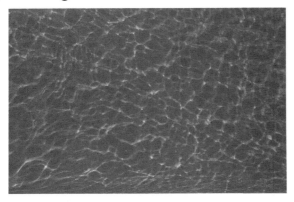

WATER

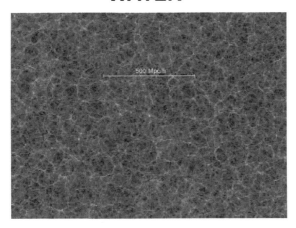

UNIVERSE

I just wanted to point out that it's important that we take God's word literally as our guideline and then see what we observe to verify His word - and not the other way around.

By applying this very sound biblical advice, we can go on to make amazing discoveries and prove that there is, in fact, a gap between Genesis 1:1 and Genesis 1:2.

CHAPTER 2
THE ALPHA AND THE OMEGA

We know that the Bible says in the beginning was the word. We also know that this Word is Jesus Christ. This is the reason the Word is living and powerful.

There is great depth to God's word. Most Christians realize that they can read the Bible several times through and get something new out of it every time.

When we realize that the Alpha and the Omega is also the Living Word, we find that the Bible often has the past and the future within the same scriptures. Ezekiel 28 is a good example of this. In the plain text, it is talking about God's judgment against the king of Tyre, but it also mentions the anointed cherub that covereth which was on the holy mountain of God.

This is obviously not the king of Tyre. It is now making reference to Satan who was formerly known as Lucifer.

It goes on to describe details about Lucifer before he fell.

What we have here is a future prophecy against the king of Tyre in the same text as the past, with Lucifer and the time that he became prideful and fell - in other words, when iniquity was found in Lucifer. Let's take a look:

Ezekiel 28:1-22 KJV

1 *The word of the Lord came again unto me, saying,*

2 *Son of man, say unto the prince of Tyrus, Thus saith the Lord God; Because thine heart is lifted up, and thou hast said, I am a God, I sit in the seat of God, in the midst of the seas; yet thou art a man, and not God, though thou set thine heart as the heart of God:*

3 *Behold, thou art wiser than Daniel; there is no secret that they can hide from thee:*

4 *With thy wisdom and with thine understanding thou hast gotten thee riches, and hast gotten gold and silver into thy treasures:*

5 *By thy great wisdom and by thy traffic hast thou increased thy riches, and thine heart is lifted up because of thy riches:*

6 *Therefore thus saith the Lord God; Because thou hast set thine heart as the heart of God;*

7 *Behold, therefore I will bring strangers upon thee, the terrible of the nations: and they shall draw their swords against the beauty of thy wisdom, and they shall defile thy brightness.*

8 *They shall bring thee down to the pit, and thou shalt die the deaths of them that are slain in the midst of the seas.*

9 *Wilt thou yet say before him that slayeth thee, I am God? but thou shalt be a man, and no God, in the hand of him that slayeth thee.*

10 *Thou shalt die the deaths of the uncircumcised by the hand of strangers: for I have spoken it, saith the Lord God.*

11 *Moreover the word of the Lord came unto me, saying,*

12 *Son of man, take up a lamentation upon the king of Tyrus, and say unto him, Thus saith the Lord God; Thou sealest up the sum, full of wisdom, and perfect in beauty.*

13 *Thou hast been in Eden the garden of God; every precious stone was thy covering, the sardius, topaz, and the diamond, the beryl, the* *onyx, and the jasper, the sapphire, the emerald, and the carbuncle, and gold: the workmanship of thy tabrets and of thy pipes was prepared in thee in the day that thou wast created.*

14 *Thou art the anointed cherub that covereth; and I have set thee so: thou wast upon the holy mountain of God; thou hast walked up and down in the midst of the stones of fire.*

15 *Thou wast perfect in thy ways from the day that thou wast created, till iniquity was found in thee.*

16 *By the multitude of thy merchandise they have filled the midst of thee with violence, and thou hast sinned: therefore I will cast thee as profane out of the mountain of God: and I will destroy thee, O covering cherub, from the midst of the stones of fire.*

17 *Thine heart was lifted up because of thy beauty, thou hast corrupted thy wisdom by reason of thy brightness: I will cast thee to the ground, I will lay thee before kings, that they may behold thee.*

18 *Thou hast defiled thy sanctuaries by the multitude of thine iniquities, by the iniquity of* *thy traffick; therefore will I bring forth a fire from the midst of thee, it shall devour thee, and I will bring thee to ashes upon the earth in the sight of all them that behold thee.*

19 *All they that know thee among the people shall be astonished at thee: thou shalt be a terror, and never shalt thou be any more.*

20 *Again the word of the Lord came unto me, saying,*

21 *Son of man, set thy face against Zidon, and prophesy against it,*

22 *And say, Thus saith the Lord God; Behold, I am against thee, O Zidon; and I will be glorified in the midst of thee: and they shall know that I am the Lord, when I shall have executed judgments in her, and shall be sanctified in her.*

This is just one example where the past and the future are mentioned in the same verse group.

The repeating pattern that I have discovered in scripture is the fall of Lucifer being mentioned in the same text as a future prophetic judgment against a person or country. Often times the country is Israel. We find an example of this in Jeremiah 4.

Most Bible scholars agree that Jeremiah 4 is a prophetic judgment against Israel that will happen in the future. However, when we read verses 23-28 it says the same thing that we read in Genesis 1:2, almost verbatim. Verse 23 starts by saying that the earth was without form and void, and verse 28 mentions this as the reason for the 95% darkness we observe in our universe. Let's take a look.

Jeremiah 4:23-28 KJV

23 *I beheld the earth, and, lo, it was without form, and void; and the heavens, and they had no light.*

24 *I beheld the mountains, and, lo, they trembled, and all the hills moved lightly.*

25 *I beheld, and, lo, there was no man, and all the birds of the heavens were fled.*

26 *I beheld, and, lo, the fruitful place was a wilderness, and all the cities thereof were broken down at the presence of the Lord, and by his fierce anger.*

27 *For thus hath the Lord said, The whole land shall be desolate; yet will I not make a full end.*

28 *For this shall the earth mourn, and the heavens above be black; because I have spoken it, I have purposed it, and will not repent, neither will I turn back from it.*

We see that verse 23 says that whatever caused the earth to become formless and void also caused the heavens to have no light. God is light, and His glory previously filled all creation. At this point, God has removed His glory. Verse 25 mentions that there was no man. Both light and man are mentioned because both previously existed and have now been removed.

In verse 27, God says that He will *not make a full end.* A full end to what? This is when the first earth age ended. This is why the creation account of our current age started with darkness and a formless and void earth.

Since when do you start a check by writing "void" across it? You write "void" after something goes wrong.

Something went wrong in the first age and this is the reason we have entropy. Everything now moves towards chaos, decline, and eventual death.

This is the reason the creation of our current age started out in darkness. This is confirmed in the very next verse.

28 *For this shall the earth mourn, and the heavens above be black; because I have spoken it, I have purposed it, and will not repent, neither will I turn back from it.*

This is another example of the past and the future mentioned within the same group of verses. Once again, we find a judgment that occurred when Lucifer fell along with a prophecy.

Isaiah 50 is yet another example of a prophecy that also mentions God's judgment against the first age that occurred when Lucifer fell.

This chapter is a prophecy of the rejection of the Jews, for their neglect and contempt of the Messiah, but it also mentions that there was *"no man"* and goes on to say that God *clothed the heavens with blackness.*

Isaiah 50:2-3 KJV

2 Wherefore, when I came, was there no man? when I called, was there none to answer?

Is my hand shortened at all, that it cannot redeem? or have I no power to deliver? behold, at my rebuke I dry up the sea, I make the rivers a wilderness: their fish stinketh, because there is no water, and dieth for thirst.

3 *I clothe the heavens with blackness, and I make sackcloth their covering.*

This was the end of the first age right after Lucifer's fall. It is saying the same thing we read in Jeremiah 4.

For those who may be thinking this is all just a series of strange coincidences we can go back to earlier verses in Jeremiah where it even mentions the land being made desolate and sackcloth.

Jeremiah 4:7-8 KJV

7 *The lion is come up from his thicket, and the destroyer of the Gentiles is on his way; he is gone forth from his place to make thy land desolate; and thy cities shall be laid waste, without an inhabitant.*

8 *For this gird you with sackcloth, lament and howl: for the fierce anger of the Lord is not turned back from us.*

Take note that Isaiah 50:2 and Jeremiah 4:25 both mention that there was no man, but you will never find any scripture reference saying that man died in the first age. In fact, it is at this time that God mentions His redemption plan for man.

Isaiah 50:2 KJV

Wherefore, when I came, was there no man? when I called, was there none to answer? Is my hand shortened at all, that it cannot redeem? or have I no power to deliver? ...

There is a lot of new revelation that is surfacing regarding the Bible.

Some things I am going to mention will not make sense to you until later on in the book. So please take notes and bear with me for now.

This veil of darkness that God placed over the universe when Lucifer fell is the Law/Torah.

This is the reason that man was not penalized, during the first age, for his rebellion. Since the Law was not in place, their sins were not yet held against them.

Romans 5:13 KJV

For until the law sin was in the world: but sin is not imputed when there is no law.

There are many examples of past judgments along with future prophetic judgments throughout the Bible. Several of these mention the fall of Lucifer and the destruction of the first earth age as was demonstrated in Ezekiel, Jeremiah, and Isaiah.

This makes sense when we understand that Jesus is the Word and He is also the Alpha and Omega, or the beginning and the end. In His word, we find the beginning and the end in the same areas of scripture.

Pay attention when you see "whole message" defined later in this book.

God's Word is His whole message to mankind. The following is an excerpt from the book Cosmic Codes written by Dr. Chuck Missler:

"One way to authenticate the *message* is to demonstrate that its source is from outside our time domain. God declares, 'I alone know the end from the beginning.' "His message includes history written in advance. This is called 'prophecy."

"An illustrative example is that of a parade. As we might sit on the curb and observe the many bands, marching units, floats, and other elements coming around the corner and passing in front of us, the parade is - to us - clearly a sequence of events."

"However, to someone who is outside the plane of the parade's existence - say, in a helicopter above the city - the beginning and the end can be simultaneously in view."

Now the question is, is there any observable historical evidence left over today that we can use to verify God's judgment over the first age when Lucifer fell?

We will address this in the next chapter.

CHAPTER 3
THE EVIDENCE IN OUR SOLAR SYSTEM

If there was a previous earth age that God destroyed, one would think that there would be some tell-tale signs of this massive destruction in our solar system.

Before we go searching for these signs, it will help us to first establish whom God gave the very exalted position of being in charge of this first age.

Once we have correctly identified the entity that was placed in charge of this first creation by God, we can go on to recognize the patterns in the destruction that occurred, and even understand why God destroyed the first age.

You probably already guessed that the being we are talking about is Lucifer. He was given a very exalted position as the covering cherub.

Ezekiel 28:14 KJV

Thou art the anointed cherub that covereth;

and I have set thee so: thou wast upon the holy mountain of God; thou hast walked up and down in the midst of the stones of fire.

At this point in time, Lucifer covered the throne, or mercy seat, of God. We actually have historical evidence of this that we can still observe today.

We will get to that evidence later in this book. For now, we will be searching for evidence in our solar system.

The Bible indicates that Lucifer was in charge of the nations that existed during the first age. When Lucifer became prideful, he influenced these nations to rebel against the Lord. When the Bible makes reference to this event, it uses the past tense "didst" or did. This is an event that already occurred.

Isaiah 14:12 KJV

How art thou fallen from heaven, O Lucifer, son of the morning! how art thou cut down to the ground, which didst weaken the nations!

We know Lucifer had already fallen when he tempted Eve in the garden.

At this time, he was known as Satan. The first age was lit by God's Glory or Spirit, and it was beautiful. When Lucifer fell, God placed a veil of darkness over our current reality/universe and separated heaven and the fullness of His glory from the rest of the universe. He then cast Lucifer down from heaven to earth and into the 95% darkness that we observe today in our universe.

There were three planets that Lucifer had dominion over before he fell. Rahab, (meaning *pride, boaster*) that is also known as Astera and was Lucifer's home planet.

Then there was Mars and Earth. God destroyed Rahab when Lucifer took on pride. God literally dashed Rahab into pieces.

The closest neighboring planet, Mars, was devastated when it was hit by several pieces of Rahab. We can also see the leftover effects of this event when we look at all the ancient craters on the moon.

The earth was also hit by these meteorites.

The most famous, and largest, of these is the one that impacted the coastline of Mexico.

It is thought to be at least six miles in diameter. The initial impact would have caused a heat wave that would have been devastating and would have likely caused the oceans to evaporate. Let's take another look at what Isaiah has to say regarding this event.

Isaiah 50:2-3 KJV

2 *Wherefore, when I came, was there no man? when I called, was there none to answer? Is my hand shortened at all, that it cannot redeem? or have I no power to deliver? behold, at my rebuke I dry up the sea, I make the rivers a wilderness: their fish stinketh, because there is no water, and dieth for thirst.*

3 *I clothe the heavens with blackness, and I make sackcloth their covering.*

Take notice that it says this occurred *"at my rebuke"*.

Who was God rebuking here? He was rebuking the fugitive snake - or Satan.

There is biblical evidence for this. This evidence also states that the heavens used to be beautiful and that God dashed the planet Rahab into pieces. Let's take a look.

Job 26:11-13 KJV 1900

"The pillars of heaven are stunned at His rebuke. He quiets the sea with his power,

and by his understanding He shatters (maw-khats, dashes asunder), Rahab, by His spirit the heavens were beautiful; His hand forbids the fugitive snake."

Psalm 89:10 KJV

Thou hast broken Rahab in pieces, as one that is slain; thou hast scattered thine enemies with thy strong arm.

Psalm 18:7 KJV

Then the earth shook and trembled; the foundations also of the hills moved and were shaken, because he was wroth.

2 Samuel 22:8 KJV

Then the earth shook and trembled; the foundations of heaven moved and shook, because he was wroth.

Let's see if there are any more observations we can make in our solar system that confirm the verses we just read.

God dashed the planet Rahab, or Astera, into pieces. We have a debris field in our solar system located between Mars and Jupiter. This is what we would expect to see if there was once a planet located in that area that exploded in the ancient past.

This is known as the Asteroid belt.

The following is an excerpt from
http://thewatcherfiles.com/rahab.htm

The accepted theory for the creation of the asteroid belt is "failed planet accretion" -- that during the primordial beginning of the solar system a planet which astronomers call Astera was forming in the place now occupied by the asteroid belt, but because of its insufficient mass, and due to Jupiter's gravitational influence, it fragmented.

This theory cannot be correct, as it is becoming obvious that both the planet Mars and the mysterious parent planet of the asteroid belt once sustained oceans and atmospheres.

This parent planetary body was broken up in a cataclysm of biblical proportions.

In the 1987 October edition of Science magazine, D.P.Cruikshank and R.H. Brown reported a startling piece of news. They had discovered organic compounds on three asteroids: Murray, 103 Electra and Orguiel.

Utilizing the process of spectral analyses of reflected light from these three asteroids,

Cruikshank and Brown detected amino acids.

More startlingly, "aqueous alteration products" such as clay were found, suggesting that the parent body had been affected by water.

If these asteroids did, in fact, contain sediment, it could not have been deposited without large quantities of liquid water laid down over a length of time.

This would have also required an environment of gravitation strong enough to hold a dense atmosphere, producing weather and water erosion.

The evidence found on these asteroids could only mean that they were from a parent body possessing an atmosphere and oceans.

The explosion on this planet would have sent several high-speed projectiles towards its nearest neighboring planet Mars, destroying all life on Mars. And as we observe Mars today it has over 80% of its impact craters on one side.

Most experts agree that this all occurred within a very short time frame, most likely half an hour.

The Mars environment was left a wasteland due to the effects of the nearby exploding Astera.

In the book *Dark Matter, Missing Planets & New Comets,* Van Flandern states that the parent body of the asteroids once sustained oceans and an atmosphere. If a planet exploded between Mars and Jupiter with enormous energy, there would initially be debris all over the solar system.

However, in just 100,000 years or so, Jupiter and the other planets swept up or ejected almost all the debris, except for the pieces between Mars and Jupiter which can never come close to any planet.

This is where the surviving minor planets are found today.

The orbits of minor planets (and comets) show imprints of an explosion event.

We have learned what such imprints look like from studying man-made satellites of the earth in a few cases where one of them has exploded.

Other evidence comes from meteors from space which reach the ground without burning up and are recovered for study, where one can see firsthand what sort of material the planet was made of.

From the tracks of cosmic rays in these meteorites, we have learned that they have been traveling in space only some millions of years, a small fraction of the age of the solar system.

Some of them show evidence of rapid melting a long time ago as if they were affected by an immense heat blast. A few show evidence of shock. Others are badly charred.

David Flynn, in His book *Cydonia: The Secret Chronicles of Mars*, mentions one of Jupiter's moons that was likely near the exploding Astera.

This moon is in a fixed orbit. This means one side is always facing Jupiter and the other side always faces the asteroid belt. It is charred black on the half that would have been facing Astera, and perfectly ok on the side facing Jupiter.

There are several other photos of the surface of Mars that show ancient structures on or just below the surface.

The Bible clearly says that the heavens were lit by God's glory and they were beautiful.

The earth did not start out formless and void,

and God did not create it in vain. He created it to be inhabited from the beginning.

When was the beginning?

Genesis 1:1 Literally says, *"In the beginning God created the heaven and the earth"*.

Scripture verifies that something occurred between Genesis 1:1 and 1:2.

Isaiah 45:18 KJV

For thus saith the Lord that created the heavens; God himself that formed the earth and made it; he hath established it,he created it not in vain, he formed it to be inhabited: I am the Lord; and there is none else.

God caused the earth to become without form and void. The beauty of God's perfect redemption plan for mankind is that this was not just a judgment against Lucifer/Satan, but a chance for us to be set free through Jesus Christ. You will see exactly how this plays out as part of God's plan down to the finest details with scripture used in the correct context.

Romans 8:20-22 ESV

20 *For the creation was subjected to futility, not willingly, but because of him who* *subjected it, in hope*

21 *that the creation itself will be set free from its bondage to corruption and obtain the freedom of the glory of the children of God.*

22 *For we know that the whole creation has been groaning together in the pains of childbirth until now.*

When did creation start *"groaning together"*?

When God placed the veil of darkness over our universe.

Jeremiah 4:28 KJV

For this shall the earth mourn, and the heavens above be black: because I have spoken it, I have purposed it, and will not repent, neither will I turn back from it.

So, what was this veil of darkness and why would God start our current age by surrounding or framing our universe with it?

This veil of darkness is the Perfect Law or the Word of God.

Hebrews 11:3 KJV

Through faith we understand that the worlds were framed by the word of God, so that things which are seen were not made of things which do appear.

CHAPTER 4
THE PERFECT LAW

Once we understand the full encompassment of what the Perfect Law is, and what it does in our current age, we will begin to understand all those different Bible passages and verses that never seemed to make sense previously.

Since the law is perfect and we live in a fallen universe, the law brings entropy on all creation in our current age. It causes things to slowly decline, break down, and eventually die. Remember what we read in Jeremiah 4:28, *"For this shall the earth mourn, and the heavens above be black".*

Not only does the law bring entropy to the earth, but it also weakens our fallen flesh bodies.

Romans 8:3 KJV

For what the law could not do, in that it was weak through the flesh, God sending his own Son in the likeness of sinful flesh, and for sin, condemned sin in the flesh:

We see that God's Son, Jesus Christ,

condemned sin in the flesh. Sin without Jesus equals death. The law without Jesus also equals death because sinful man can never hope to keep God's Perfect Law.

Galatians 3:10 KJV

For as many as are of the works of the law are under the curse: for it is written, Cursed is every one that continueth not in all things which are written in the book of the law to do them.

So, we can see that those who don't have Christ as their Savior are both spiritually, and literally physically under the curse of the law. Remember that the law is the word of God that is a veil of darkness that God stretched over our universe. This would place all fallen humans literally under the law.

God's Perfect Law and Jesus Christ are in perfect harmony because the law has no negative effect on the perfect, sinless Son of God.

Since the veil of darkness, the law, was not yet in place during the first age when Lucifer weakened the nations through deception, which lead to their disobedience and rebellion against

God, their sin was not yet held against them.

When scripture is read in the correct context we will see that this is exactly what it says.

When Adam partook of the forbidden fruit he was condemned to death.

At this time God removed Adam from of a perfect environment that was in another dimension here on earth, the Garden of Eden, and He placed him in an environment that was literally under the law or veil of darkness which causes the earth to mourn and the heavens above to be black.

This new environment contained entropy which would cause Adam's body to start heading towards decline, or to begin aging, and would eventually lead to his physical death. We realize that the law brings about death, and that this actually caused Adam's physical death, and yet the Bible says that sin was not held against man until the law was put in place. There is a great mystery here that we will solve by taking God's word literally.

We have two laws, or *Torahs,* which are actually one and the same. One contains the source code that forms our reality and is described as a black veil that frames or surrounds our universe. The other is (the same law) the law that Moses received from the Lord written out in 2D (two dimensions).

Both forms of the law create veils and both veils are removed by Jesus Christ. The 2D version of the law given to Moses represents the veil that was in the temple and torn in two when Jesus paid the price for our sins and hence restored direct access to Father God for all that receive this free gift.

The law that frames our universe also creates the veil of darkness that will be removed by Jesus when He restores the heavens and earth. If you remember that this veil separates our reality from God's Glory, then you will realize that when Jesus removes it, He will also be restoring the fullness of the Father's glory to shine upon all creation from that point forward.

We must remember that this veil of darkness is the Law/Torah that was placed over our universe when Lucifer fell.

Therefore, sin started with Lucifer and entered our world from another spiritual dimension when Adam ate the fruit. Something cannot "enter" unless it already exists.

Romans 5:12-14 KJV

12 *Wherefore, as by one man sin entered into the world, and death by sin; and so death passed upon all men, for that all have sinned:*

13 *(For until the law sin was in the world: but sin is not imputed when there is no law.*

14 *Nevertheless death reigned from Adam to Moses, even over them that had not sinned after the similitude of Adam's transgression, who is the figure of him that was to come.*

Verse 13 clearly says that sin is not imputed when there is no law.

But we know Adam was sentenced when he ate the fruit. This would not make sense if one did not understand that the veil/Law/Torah was placed over our universe when Lucifer fell and later, when Adam sinned he was kicked out of a perfect environment into another dimension here on earth and placed in our current reality that is under the veil of darkness, or Law.

People mistake this for the law of Moses because Moses is mentioned in verse 14. But verse 14 is actually confirming that it isn't the law of Moses by saying that death reigned from Adam to Moses.

The wages of sin is death. Death reigned from Adam to Moses and yet sin is not imputed when there is no law.

For death to reign from Adam to Moses, it is clear that sin was imputed before Moses, and therefore there was a Law in place before Moses was given the 2D Torah.

To further simplify this issue, one only need to ask if Adam's partaking of the fruit was considered a transgression and was Adam was punished for this transgression?

Genesis 2:17 KJV

> *But of the tree of the knowledge of good and evil, thou shalt not eat of it: for in the day that thou eatest thereof thou shalt surely die.*

We know Adam ate the fruit, so he definitely committed a transgression and we know the wages of sin is death; *"in the day that thou eatest thereof thou shalt surely die."* So we know there was an extreme penalty for Adam's sin and that his sin was counted.

I will give a couple more verses that are very hard to rectify unless you realize that there was a previous earth age and a Law/Torah, or veil of darkness over the universe.

Romans 4:15 ESV

For the law brings wrath, but where there is no law there is no transgression.

Romans 5:13 ESV

for sin indeed was in the world before the law was given, but sin is not counted where there is no law.

Jeremiah 4:28 KJV

For this shall the earth mourn, and the heavens above be black; because I have spoken it, I have purposed it, and will not repent, neither will I turn back from it.

In Romans chapter 7, Paul talks about the law.

He goes on to mention the first earth age and that he was alive once until the law was put in place and then he died.

We know Paul was physically alive when he made that statement. This implies that Paul was making reference to his spirit. We are born with living souls but with dead spirits because we are born under the law/veil when we enter our current age. Let's take a look at what Paul said.

Romans 7:9 KJV

For I was alive without the law once: but when the commandment came, sin revived, and I died.

This has profound implications when one realizes that sin was not imputed until the law was put over the universe when Lucifer fell. How do we know there was a previous age in which God placed Lucifer in charge, and that some form of humans was there and they actually sinned?

Isaiah 14:12 KJV

How art thou fallen from heaven, O Lucifer, son of the morning! how art thou cut down to the ground, which didst weaken the nations!

We know for a fact Lucifer was already fallen when he tempted Eve in the garden. *"which didst* (or *did*, past tense) *weaken the nations"*. At this point it clearly says that Lucifer had already weakened the nations. In other words, Lucifer caused the nations to rebel or sin.

This sin was not counted against them because the first age was lit by God's glory.

This means the law/Torah/veil of darkness was

not put in place yet. Remember, God put this veil/Law in place in our current age and reality as a judgment against Lucifer when Lucifer tried to exalt himself to the level of God.

It is also important to consider that the tree that God commanded them not to eat of is called "the tree of the knowledge of good and evil".

In the same way that something cannot enter unless it already exists (sin), you cannot have knowledge of something that does not exist.

Eating from the forbidden tree simply made them aware of something that already existed since the rebellion of Lucifer, which was "evil".

When we understand God's word in the correct context, everything will make sense. However, when we don't get the context and/or meaning correct, God's word can appear inaccurate at best, and totally contradicting in worse-case scenarios.

I will give a good example of this that pertains to the garden of Eden. Satan told Eve that she would not surely die when she ate the forbidden fruit.

Genesis 3:4 KJV

And the serpent said unto the woman, Ye

shall not surely die:

And yet we know that God told them that the same day they ate the fruit they would die.

Genesis 2:17 KJV

But of the tree of the knowledge of good and evil, thou shalt not eat of it: for in the day that thou eatest thereof thou shalt surely die.

We also know that Adam and Eve were kicked out of the garden and went on to live several hundred more years. At first glance, this would seem to make Satan's statement more correct than what God told them. This is why it is critical to look at the details of scripture in context.

We know the first sin was committed by Lucifer in the previous age.

When Adam ate the fruit, he opened a spiritual portal that allowed sin to "enter". Something cannot enter unless it already exists.

Romans 5:12 KJV

Wherefore, as by one man sin entered into the world, and death by sin; and so death passed upon all men, for that all have sinned:

We know *the wages of sin is death.* The day sin entered, Adam's spirit died. The interesting thing is, if you take this verse literally it says, *"all have sinned"* - past tense.

There is another verse that says the same thing and, once again, uses the past tense.

Romans 3:23 ESV

"For all have sinned and fall short of the glory of God."

This verse does not say that all will eventually sin. It clearly says that everyone already has sinned. This will make sense in the most literal way as we learn more about this.

Remember that I pointed out that the Bible is a lot more literal than most people realize.

The verse goes on to say that all have fallen short of God's glory. You will learn that this too is very literal. I would advise that you take notes at this point to reference and compare later on in this book.

This has profound implications that we will look into a little later.

What I want to point out is that Adam cannot pass his spirit on, but he can and did reproduce and pass on the fallen flesh that eventually dies.

Death of the flesh is what Adam passed on. Through Adam's offense sin entered our reality and therefore through Adam's offense we are born with corrupted fallen bodies that die. This is verified in 1 Corinthians 15:50.

Corinthians 15:50 KJV

Now this I say, brethren, that flesh and blood cannot inherit the kingdom of God; neither doth corruption inherit incorruption.

What is corrupt? Flesh and blood. The flesh of all mankind is condemned to die through Adam.

Remember that the Perfect Law brings entropy to a fallen flesh body. Once Adam sinned he was cast out of the garden of Eden and he entered the fallen dimension that is under the law.

Romans 5 covers everything we just went over and the second to the last verse in this chapter is Romans 5:20. Let's take a look:

Romans 5:20 KJV

Moreover the law entered, that the offence might abound. But where sin abounded, grace did much more abound:

Let's consider what that verse actually implies. The Law was put in place because of the offense.

The law already existed outside the garden of Eden. It was in place before Adam ever sinned. The law was in place to take its toll on sin before Adam ever committed the offense.

This is implying that the offense already occurred.

The offence was the rebellion that happened in the first earth age. This also implies that Adam was a divine set up to serve a greater cause, pertaining to a much bigger picture, that most people are unaware of.

This is confirmed when we realize that Adam was made from the dust of the earth, or *"flesh and blood"*. The Bible says flesh and blood cannot inherit the kingdom of God.

I have often wondered why the first man would fall right out of the starting gate, especially when one considers that Adam actually walked with God in the garden. It would make more sense if a distant descendant of Adam who did not have such a direct relationship with the Lord would have been the one to eat the fruit.

The Bible actually lets us know that this was a divine setup. God already had it all planned out. This is why Christ was already chosen to redeem us before Adam ever sinned.

1 Peter 1:20 KJV

Who verily was foreordained before the foundation of the world, but was manifest in these last times for you,

We need to realize that amazing biblical info is just surfacing that has previously been overlooked, misunderstood, or taken out of context during these end times that we currently live in as per Daniel 12:4:

Daniel 12:4 KJV

But thou, O Daniel, shut up the words, and seal the book, even to the time of the end: many shall run to and fro, and knowledge shall be increased.

CHAPTER 5
THE GREAT PYRAMID

(A Testimony of the First Earth Age)

If you were to ask most Christians how old they think the earth is, you would likely discover that most of the answers would be between 6,000 and 9,000 years old.

There is a great mystery here that needs to be solved in order to truly understand reality, the age of the earth, and the different earth ages.

One thing that has been the topic of many heated debates is the dating methods that are currently being used, and their accuracy. For example, they claim that ice-core samples taken in Antarctica date as old as 2.7 million years.

The following is an excerpt from *www.sciencemag.org:*

Record-shattering 2.7-million-year-old ice core reveals start of the ice ages

Scientists announced today that a core drilled in Antarctica has yielded 2.7-million-year-old ice, an astonishing find 1.7 million years older than the previous record-holder.

Bubbles in the ice contain greenhouse gases from Earth's atmosphere at a time when the planet's cycles of glacial advance and retreat were just beginning, potentially offering clues to what triggered the ice ages. That information alone makes the value of the sample "incredible," says David Shuster, a geochemist at the University of California, Berkeley, who is unaffiliated with the research. "This is the only sample of ancient Earth's atmosphere that we have access to."

Other "experts" date Antarctica's ice to 35 million years old.

The following is an excerpt from *www.ancient-code.com:*

"According to scientists, ICE in Antarctica 'suddenly appeared' some 35 million years ago. One hundred million years before that, the continent remained free of ice."

Despite what the experts claim there is information that completely contradicts these extremely old ages given for Antarctica's ice.

The following is an excerpt from
http://www.collective-evolution.com:

500 YEAR OLD MAP WAS DISCOVERED THAT SHATTERS THE "OFFICIAL" HISTORY OF THE PLANET.

"Human history is quite an enigma. We know so little, and much of what we think we know is always subject to change since information constantly emerges that challenges our current understanding of the world."

Our world is also no stranger to unexplained mysteries, and there are numerous examples of verified phenomena, ancient monuments, books, teachings, understandings, and more that lack any explanation and counter what we've already been taught.

We are like a race with amnesia, (Interestingly enough, this statement will be confirmed in Job 8:8-9 KJV, later on in this book- Author's note) able to put together small bits and pieces of our history yet unable to fit it all together. There are still many missing pieces to the puzzle.

One great example is the Piri Reis map, a genuine document that was copied at Constantinople in AD 1513 from older documents and discovered in 1929. It focuses on the western coast of Africa, the eastern coast of South America, and the northern coast of Antarctica.

It was drawn by Admiral Piri Reis of the Ottoman era, a well-known historical figure. He made a copy of the map, which was originally drawn based ondocuments that date back to at least the fourth century BC, and on information obtained by multiple explorers.

Why the map Is so compelling?

One of the most compelling facts about the map is that it includes a continent that our history books tell us was not discovered until 1818.

Secondly, the map depicts what is known as "Queen Maud Land," a 2.7 million-square-kilometer (1 million sq. mi.) region of Antarctica as it looked millions of years ago.

This region and other regions shown on the map are thought to have been covered completely in ice, but the map tells a different story, showing them free of ice, which suggests they passed through a long ice-free period that may not have ended until around six thousand years ago, conflicting with current research on these areas.

Today, geological evidence has confirmed that this area could not have been ice-free until about 4000 BC.

Official science has been saying all along that the icecap which covers the Antarctic is millions of years old. The Piri Reis map shows that the northern part of that continent had been mapped before the ice did cover it, which means that it was mapped a million years ago — but that's impossible, since mankind did not exist at that time. Quite the conundrum, isn't it?

My point is that the dating methods used have been proven to be highly inaccurate in several cases. I won't go into all the details that show the flaws in these dating methods. If you are interested in reading about this, you can visit one or both of the links below.

More Bad News for Radiometric Dating

http://www.cs.unc.edu/~plaisted/ce/ dating2.html

The way it really is: little-known facts about radiometric dating:

Long-age geologists will not accept a radiometric date unless it matches their pre-existing expectations.

by ***Tas Walker***

https://creation.com/the-way-it-really-is-little-known-facts-about-radiometric-dating

The Great Pyramid of Giza is one of the keys needed in order to solve this mystery regarding the age of the earth, and even the different earth ages.

The Great Pyramid is the first wonder of the world listed by the Greeks and the only remaining wonder of the seven original wonders of the world.

It has been studied through the ages leaving its observers in awe and wonder at is size and precision.

When was this pyramid built and for what purpose? I believe the keys to solving this mystery lay within the pages of another ancient wonder, the Bible.

However, the capstone was never completed. To this day the capstone (if it existed it would be 30 ft. x 30 ft.) is missing.

The missing capstone will make sense as you read on. In light of recent study, I have come to the conclusion that the Great Pyramid was built as an Altar to the Lord, and a replica of the heavenly New Jerusalem, during the first earth age.

Photo shows that The Great Pyramid is missing the capstone.

Let's take a look at the evidence:

The pyramid is oriented true north with a greater accuracy than any known monument, astronomical site, or any other building. In our times, the most accurate north oriented structure is the Paris Observatory.

"It is 6 minutes of a degree off replica watches true north. The Great Pyramid of Giza is only 3 minutes of a degree off true north. Studies have shown that this 3 minutes of a degree off true north is due to either a shift in the earth's pole or movement of the African continent. It originally was perfectly oriented to true north."

Source: *http://www.gizapyramid.com/general.htm*

I believe that if we can find out what caused the pole shift that threw the pyramid three minutes of a degree off true north, we can also verify when the pyramid was constructed.

The key here is "what" caused the pole shift. With the dating methods proven to be highly inaccurate, we can't necessarily go by the dates given as they are extreme, which is usually the case when we consider the fact that most of the researchers that throw these extremely old dates out there are also the same people that support and push the theory of evolution.

So, what caused the pole shift?

There was a cataclysmic event eons ago. This is the same event that most experts think caused the extinction of the dinosaurs.

Scientists now have fresh evidence that a cosmic impact, from an asteroid or comet, ended the age of dinosaurs.

This idea was first proposed by physicist Luis Alvarez and his son geologist Walter Alvarez.

Scientists later found that signs of this collision seemed evident near the town of Chicxulub (CHEEK-sheh-loob) in Mexico in the form of a gargantuan crater more than 110 miles (180 kilometers) wide.

The explosion, likely caused by an object about 6 miles (10 km) across, would have released as much energy as 100 trillion tons of TNT, more than a billion times more than the atom bombs that destroyed Hiroshima and Nagasaki.

"We've shown the impact and the mass extinction coincided as much as one can possibly demonstrate with existing dating techniques," researcher Paul Renne, a geochronologist, and director of the Berkeley Geochronology Center in California told LiveScience.

There was an event, recorded in the Bible, that happened eons ago, that accounts for the asteroid impact that caused the pole shift.

God placed Lucifer in charge of the first creation before Lucifer's fall. Likely because of Lucifer's great beauty, intelligence, and the high position God placed him in, Lucifer became filled with pride and made the following statements:

Isaiah 14:13-14 KJV

13 *For thou hast said in thine heart, "I will ascend into heaven, I will exalt my throne above the stars of God: I will sit also upon the mount of the congregation, in the sides of the north:*

14 *I will ascend above the heights of the clouds; I will be like the most High."*

As far as I have ever known, if someone has a throne, they also have a kingdom.

The three known planets Lucifer had dominion over were Earth, Mars and Astera a.k.a. Rahab or Tiamet.

Now let's do a quick review:

Astera underwent a catastrophic explosion in the distant past.

Some estimate ten to twenty thousand years ago and some place a far greater age on the occurrence of this event. The remains of this explosion left behind what we now refer to as the Asteroid Belt.

When Satan and his angels rebelled, God destroyed their literal dwelling places. According to scripture, this destruction was swift and decisive.

 The fifth terrestrial planet which God calls "Rahab" *(boaster, pride)*, was obliterated.

Job 26:11-13

"The pillars of heaven are stunned at His rebuke. He quiets The sea with his power, - and by his understanding He shatters (maw-khats, dashes asunder), Rahab, -by His spirit the heavens were beautiful; His hand forbids the fugitive snake."

The explosion on this planet would have sent several highspeed projectiles towards its

nearest neighboring planet Mars, destroying all life on Mars.

And as we observe Mars today, it has over 80% of its impact craters on one side. Most experts agree that this all occurred within a very short time frame, most likely half an hour.

The Mars environment was left a wasteland due to the effects of the nearby exploding Astera.

There are several other photos of the surface of Mars that show ancient structures on or just below the surface. This explains the famous 'face' on Mars.

This event also gives a good explanation for the craters we see on the moon.

I believe this event caused the aforementioned impact on earth and the resulting pole shift, which in turn threw the Great Pyramid off by 3 degrees.

This happened right before God placed the veil of darkness over our universe.

The meteorite from Rahab that hit earth threw the *foundations of the earth out of course.* This is why our current earth's axis tilts at 23.5 degrees.

Psalm 82:5 KJV

5 They know not, neither will they understand; they walk on in darkness: all the foundations of the earth are out of course.

This dates the Great Pyramid back to the first earth age.

My studies show that the first earth age was not just a different period of time, but it actually had a different makeup of reality at the quantum level.

I will give the evidence for this later on in the book, but I mentioned it here because I believe our current age is between 6,000 and 8,000 years old.

Therefore, if the Great Pyramid was under construction towards the end of the first age, as the following evidence shows, it would appear to be around 9,000 years old.

I say "appear" because the amount of time between the first age ending and the creation of our current age is uncertain though the Bible seems to indicate that God emediately started our current age after the first earth age ended. Take note of this now because this evidence is found in the last chapter of this book.

It is also uncertain if and how things would age (during the gap between the ages) since the transition from the first age to our current age involves different forms of reality.

To narrow this mystery down further, we need to find out why the Great Pyramid was built.

I believe the Great Pyramid was built to be the earthly replica of the heavenly New Jerusalem.

The Bible describes its size and lay-out.

Revelation 21:1-3 and 15-17 (KJV)

1 And I saw a new heaven and a new earth: for the first heaven and the first earth were passed away; and there was no more sea.

2 And I John saw the holy city, new Jerusalem, coming down from God out of heaven, prepared as a bride adorned for her husband.

3 And I heard a great voice out of heaven saying, Behold, the tabernacle of God is with men, and he will dwell with them, and they shall be his people, and God himself shall be with them, and be their God

15 And he that talked with me had a golden reed to measure the city, and the gates thereof, and the wall thereof.

16 *And the city lieth foursquare, and the length is as large as the breadth: and he measured the city with the reed, twelve thousand furlongs. The length and the breadth and the height of it are equal.*

17 *And he measured the wall thereof, an hundred and forty and four cubits, according to the measure of a man, that is, of the angel.*

According to these measurements many people have mistakenly assumed that the New Jerusalem is a giant cube, however, the same measurements can apply to a pyramid, and the pyramid fits into the big picture and the grand scheme of things and lines up with Bible prophecy in several ways whereas a giant cube just doesn't seem to fit.

The description of New Jerusalem states that *"the city lieth foursquare, and the length is as large as the breadth: and he measured the city with the reed, twelve thousand furlongs. The length and the breadth and the height of it are equal."*

The key to understanding the true shape lays within the details of the description in context.

"... the city LIETH foursquare".

This is making reference to the base or the part that lays on the ground.

A pyramid lieth foursquare, but a cube is squared regardless whether you are talking about the top, side or bottom. This was thought of as being a giant cube before, but keep in mind that Christ is the chief cornerstone that the builders rejected.

Matthew 21:42

Jesus saith unto them, Did ye never read in the scriptures, The stone which the builders rejected, the same is become the head of the corner: this is the Lord's doing, and it is marvellous in our eyes?

Psalm 118:22

The stone which the builders refused is become the head stone of the corner

Mark 12:10

And have ye not read this scripture; The stone which the builders rejected is become the head of the corner:

The cornerstone (or foundation stone) concept is derived from the first stone set in the construction of a masonry foundation, important since all other stones will be set in reference to this stone, thus determining the position of the entire structure.

It seems to me that the chief cornerstone would be where all corners met.

In a cube, this doesn't fit, but if the top four corners were to all meet at the same place, the shape would change from a cube to a pyramid, yet keeping all the dimensions given in scripture.

Relating back to Christ being the chief cornerstone, notice in a pyramid shape that the capstone consists of four corners all meeting in one place - the top. That would make Him the capstone of the pyramid shape. Relate that to the body of Christ. He is the head [capstone] and we (as Christians) are all the body [base] of the pyramid.

I also want to remind you that the Great Pyramid of Giza is missing its capstone.

The New Jerusalem will descend from heaven to earth during the future and final earth age. It will radiate with the Glory of God. I believe this is due to the highly reflective makeup of the New Jerusalem and the fact that the veil of darkness that currently covers our universe (as God's judgement due to the fall of Satan) will have been removed by Jesus and all creation will be lit by God's Glory that is beyond the veil.

The Bible mentions this veil in several places. I will give a couple examples.

Isaiah 50:3

I clothe the heavens with blackness, and I make sackcloth their covering.

Isaiah 40:22

It is he that sitteth upon the circle of the earth, and the inhabitants thereof are as grasshoppers; that stretcheth out the heavens as a curtain, and spreadeth them out as a tent to dwell in:

The Bible also mentions the New Jerusalem descending from heaven and radiating with God's Glory.

Revelation 21:10 KJV

And he carried me away in the spirit to a great and high mountain, and shewed me that great city, the holy Jerusalem, descending out of heaven from God.

Revelation 21:23 KJV

And the city had no need of the sun, neither of the moon, to shine in it: for the glory of God did lighten it, and the Lamb is the light thereof.

So, in the future, the New Jerusalem will sit on the earth and reflect the Glory of God that will shine down on it after the veil is removed.

We can obviously see that the Great Pyramid, as it is today, does not shine or reflect much at all.

So, if it if it was designed to be a replica of the New Jerusalem it would necessarily have to have reflected and shone brilliantly at some point. But is there any evidence to support this?

"ORIGINAL CONSTRUCTION MADE THE PYRAMID SHINE LIKE A STAR"

It was originally covered with casing stones (made of highly polished limestone).

These casing stones reflected the sun's light and made the pyramid shine like a jewel.

They are no longer presently being used by Arabs to build mosques since an earthquake in the 14th century loosened many of them.

It has been calculated that the original pyramid with its casing stones would act like gigantic mirrors and reflect light so powerful that it would be visible from the moon as a shining star on earth. Appropriately, the ancient Egyptians called the Great Pyramid *"Ikhet"*, meaning the *"Glorious Light"*.

Source: *www.gizapyramid.com*

The Heavenly New Jerusalem is the City of God where Jesus went to prepare a place for Christians, and I would suspect this is also where God sits on the mercy seat of the heavenly Ark of the Covenant.

So, one would think that an earthly replica would also have a place for the earthly Ark of the Covenant. Let's examine this.

Inside the King's Chamber of the pyramid is a stone coffer (initiation box) with the exact dimensions of the biblical Ark of the Covenant.

Even more astounding, the stone coffer is too big to get through the door of the King's chamber, so the entire structure of the pyramid was built with this coffer in mind.

This coffer was the only furniture piece in the King's Chamber, and the Ark of the Covenant is the only piece in the Holy of Holies of God. What's more, the King's Chamber of the Great Pyramid is the same cubic volume of the bronze laver in Solomon's temple.

It seems there was an ark that predates the ark of the covenant by thousands of years and yet had the same dimensions as indicated by the empty coffer in the king's chamber.

It makes sense that there was some type of covenant between God, Lucifer, and the humanoids that existed during the first age. I say "humanoids" because we know that Adam was the first flesh and blood man that God made. See 1 Corinthians 15:45.

We will go into what and whom these "humanoids" were later in the book.

I believe the first ark would have had one cherub at the center of the mercy seat in a kneeling position with his wings spread out to either side covering the lid.

In Ezekiel 28:14 it mentions Lucifer in the singular as the covering cherub during this time period.

Ezekiel 28:14 (KJV)

14 *"Thou art the anointed cherub that covereth; and I have set thee so: thou wast upon the holy mountain of God; thou hast walked up and down in the midst of the stones of fire."*

Later on, when Moses was instructed to build the ark of the covenant, we have two cherubims covering the mercy seat. This could have been to prevent the reoccurrence of pride that happened as a result of giving one entity such an exalted position. These two cherubims could very well represent Michael and Gabriel.

The Bible mentions this in **Exodus 25: 17-20 KJV**

17 *"And thou shalt make a mercy seat of pure gold: two cubits and a half shall be the length thereof, and a cubit and a half the breadth thereof.*

18 *And thou shalt make two cherubims of gold, of beaten work shalt thou make them, in the two ends of the mercy seat.*

19 *And make one cherub on the one end, and the other cherub on the other end: even of the mercy seat shall ye make the* *cherubims on the two ends thereof.*

20 *And the cherubims shall stretch forth their wings on high, covering the mercy seat with their wings, and their faces shall look one to another; toward the mercy seat shall the faces of the cherubims be."*

God would have removed this ark (the first ark) when Lucifer fell from grace. This is another piece of evidence that points to the Great Pyramid being under construction at the end of the first earth age.

Inside, there is a broad way that leads to a pit and a narrow way that leads to the king's chamber. (Read Matthew 7.)

The 153 steps in the pyramid match the 153 fishes gathered in John 21:11, which may be a reference to all nations of the earth gathering into the kingdom of God.

The king's chamber is on the fiftieth row of the stones; 50 was the year of Jubilee (Leviticus 25:11).

Although most have been torn off, the pyramid was originally covered with 144,000 polished casing stones, the number of witnesses in

Revelation 7:4. The stones were a perfect fit such that many of the seams could not be seen nor a paper put between them today, thousands of years later.

The cornerstone at the top is missing, symbolic of Christ, the rejected chief cornerstone (Daniel 2:45; Psalm 118:22; Matthew 21:42; Mk 12:10).

The five-sided cornerstone may represent the number of grace.

The missing capstone makes sense if the pyramid was under construction during the first earth age.

When Satan rebelled, he would likely have ordered those under him to stop construction as the capstone represented Jesus Christ, and this is the very position that Satan desired for himself, even into modern times, as represented by the Eye of Horus.

Horus is Osiris, a.k.a. Lucifer. This can be seen on the back of every U.S dollar bill.

The Great Pyramid is of such magnitude that it could not be built today.

It is 90 times the volume of the Chicago Sears Tower.

Napoleon said there was enough stone in the pyramid to build a 10-foot-high brick wall all the way around France! Some stones near the top, 400 feet from the ground, weigh 70 tons!

The foundation covers so wide an area (over 13 acres) that it could not be built today as level as it is (less than 1/10-inch error in 13 acres). Every locomotive in the world harnessed to the pyramid could not budge it.

The door is so well joined that it was undetectable from the outside for centuries.

Ancient Egypt was divided into two regions, namely Upper Egypt and Lower Egypt.

To the north was Lower Egypt, where the Nile stretched out with its several branches to form the Nile Delta. To the south was Upper Egypt, stretching to Syene.

Therefore, the location of the Great Pyramid is

in the center of Egypt, on the boarder of where it is divided.

Isaiah 19:19-20 KJV

19 *In that day shall there be an altar to the Lord in the midst of the land of Egypt, and a pillar at the border thereof to the Lord.*

20 *And it shall be for a sign and for a witness unto the Lord of hosts in the land of Egypt: for they shall cry unto the Lord because of the oppressors, and he shall send them a saviour, and a great one, and he shall deliver them.*

In Hebrew, each letter has a numerical value. The Pyramid's height in inches equals the sum of all the letters in the Hebrew text of Isaiah 19:19-20 (5,449).

Conclusion

I think the evidence clearly shows that the Great Pyramid was constructed during the first earth age as a replica of the heavenly New Jerusalem.

CHAPTER 6
JESUS, THE HEAD-CORNERSTONE

We went over the fact that the Great Pyramid has been missing its capstone for all recorded history. We also went over the fact that Jesus is the Head Cornerstone or Capstone of the heavenly New Jerusalem. This would mean that the missing capstone on the Great Pyramid was intended to represent Jesus Christ.

During the first earth age when Lucifer became prideful, he ordered the builders to stop construction of the Great Pyramid because the capstone, or head position, was the very position Lucifer desired for himself. So, who were these builders? Would you believe it if I told you it was all of us that exist now in our current, and fallen earth age?

Acts 4:11 NASB

He is the Stone which was rejected by you, The Builders, but which became The Chief Corner Stone.

This will make more sense once we realize that everything in our current age is a dim, puzzling reflection of eternity and the eternal order.

1 Corinthians 13:12 NLT

Now we see things imperfectly, like puzzling reflections in a mirror, but then we will see everything with perfect clarity. All that I know now is partial and incomplete, but then I will know everything completely, just as God now knows me completely.

1 Corinthians 13:12 BSB

Now we see but a dim reflection as in a mirror; then we shall see face to face. Now I know in part; then I shall know fully, even as I am fully known.

I will demonstrate this in detail in later chapters but for now, I want to point out that Adam was a reflection of Jesus Christ, whom the Bible calls the Last Adam.

1 Corinthians 15:45 NLT

The Scriptures tell us, "The first man, Adam, became a living person." But the last Adam-- that is, Christ--is a life-giving Spirit.

We know Eve was Adam's bride just as all true Christians will become the bride of Christ.

Satan always attacks the weaker vessel. In the Garden of Eden this was Eve.

However, in the previous earth age, this was all of us, or in other words, the Builders that were deceived and rejected Jesus as the Chief or Head Cornerstone.

We made up the "nations" that Satan deceived.

Isaiah 14:12 KJV

How art thou fallen from heaven, O Lucifer, son of the morning! how art thou cut down to the ground, which didst weaken the nations!

Notice is says *"didst"* which is another word for "did" - meaning past tense. This event already happened. We know for a fact Satan had already fallen when he was in the Garden of Eden and deceived Eve.

This is verification that these *"nations"* existed in a previous age.

The Bible refers to the body, of both the Great Pyramid of Giza and the Heavenly New Jerusalem, as *"pillars"*. This is further biblical verification that the pyramid is the correct shape of the New Jerusalem and therefore it is also the correct shape that would represent Jesus as the rejected pyramid-shaped Capstone.

First, let's take a look at where the Bible makes reference to the body of the Great Pyramid as a *"pillar"*.

We already verified that Isaiah 19:19 is making reference to the Great Pyramid. Now let's take another look at this verse.

Isaiah 19:19 KJV

*In that day shall there be an altar to the Lord in the midst of the land of Egypt, and a **PILLAR** at the border thereof to the Lord.*

We know that capstone is missing and therefore we also know that "pillar" has to reference the remainder of the Great Pyramid, which is the body.

When it comes to the bride of Christ, Christians are the body, or pillar, and Jesus is the Capstone, which together make up the heavenly New Jerusalem. We can verify this by looking at Revelation 3:12.

Revelation 3:12 KJV

*Him that overcometh will I make a **PILLAR** in the temple of my God, and he shall go no more out: and I will write upon him the name of my God, and the name of the city of my God, which is new Jerusalem, which cometh* *down out of heaven from my God: and I will write upon him my new name.*

So, we enter this fallen earth age with fallen (dead) spirits and fallen fleshly bodies at the time of birth.

This is why our spirits are made alive when we ask Jesus Christ to be our Savior and are *"born again".*

If you look on the back of any U.S. one dollar bill, you will see that Satan has assumed the position as the capstone of the Great Pyramid in this fallen age.

The Eye of Horus is depicted as capping the pyramid. Horus is Osiris reincarnated and Osiris is just another name for Lucifer.

In my previous book, The Matrix Code and The Alien Agenda, I show that the Illuminati actually admit to worshipping Lucifer (the Light-Bringer) as their god.

The first earth age was lit by God's glory and represents life. The age we currently exist in is fallen and under a veil of darkness and represents death. The age to come, once Jesus removes this veil, will represent resurrection and be, once again, lit by God's glory.

All creation, in all three earth ages, revolves around Jesus Christ.

When the Bible mentions the end of the first earth age it also asks; *"Is my hand shortened at all, that it cannot redeem?"*

Isaiah 50:2-3 KJV

2. Wherefore, when I came, was there no man? when I called, was there none to answer? Is my hand shortened at all, that it cannot redeem? or have I no power to deliver? behold, at my rebuke I dry up the sea, I make the rivers a wilderness: their fish stinketh, because there is no water, and dieth for thirst.

3. I clothe the heavens with blackness, and I make sackcloth their covering.

We can verify that this is when the earth became *without form and void and darkness covered the face of the deep.*

Like Isaiah 50:2-3, there is another book in the Bible that says, *"there was no man"* and ends with this being the reason that the heavens have blackness as the backdrop to our current, fallen universe. Like Genesis 1:2, this other Bible book also starts out by saying that the earth was without form and void.

Jeremiah 4:23-28 KJV

23 *I beheld the earth, and, lo, it was without form, and void; and the heavens, and they had no light.*

24 *I beheld the mountains, and, lo, they trembled, and all the hills moved lightly.*

25 *I beheld, and, lo, there was no man, and all the birds of the heavens were fled.*

26 *I beheld, and, lo, the fruitful place was a wilderness, and all the cities thereof were broken down at the presence of the Lord, and by his fierce anger.*

27 *For thus hath the Lord said, The whole land shall be desolate; yet will I not make a full end.*

28 *For this shall the earth mourn, and the heavens above be black; because I have* *spoken it, I have purposed it, and will not repent, neither will I turn back from it.*

Notice that Isaiah 50:2 says: *"Is my hand shortened at all, that it cannot redeem? or have I no power to deliver?"* and Jeremiah 4: 27 says: *"The whole land shall be desolate; yet will I not make a full end."*

God started over with our current earth age and we are all born into it in need of redemption. His awesome plan to deliver us from our own rebellion and fall was to send Jesus Christ in the flesh. This is why Jesus was considered crucified before the foundations of our current earth age and world we exist in now.

The Bible mentions this in a few places. The first example I will give is when it is saying that everyone will worship the beast except for all true Christians.

Revelation 13:8 KJV

And all that dwell upon the earth shall worship him, whose names are not written in the book of life of the Lamb slain from the foundation of the world.

The other reference I will give actually says that

Jesus was known before this age and appeared in this age for our sake.

1 Peter 1:20 NASB

For He was foreknown before the foundation of the world, but has appeared in these last times for the sake of you.

"The foundation of the world" is making reference to the foundation of our current world. This is verified in the last chapter of this book. In Genesis 1:2, the earth became *without form and void* due to God's judgement, we can also know that the offense or rebellion happened during the first earth age and hence the reason Jesus was *"foreknown before the foundation"* of our present world.

Adam was not created until our current age, or the second earth age, and yet Christ was considered crucified from the foundations of the world for our sake, because of the offense we committed was during that time period.

Adam was part of God's redemption plan for us, and hence the reason Adam fell right out of the starting gate. It was a divine setup. We will examine this in the next chapter.

CHAPTER 7
ADAM

(A Divine Setup)

To come to the correct biblical conclusions, we need to realize who we are as the bride of Christ.

The saints will be united with Jesus during the marriage supper of the Lamb.

Revelation 19:6-9 NKJV

> 6 *And I heard, as it were, the voice of a great multitude, as the sound of many waters and as the sound of mighty thunderings, saying, "Alleluia! For the Lord God Omnipotent reigns!*
>
> 7 *Let us be glad and rejoice and give Him glory, for the marriage of the Lamb has come, and His wife has made herself ready."*
>
> 8 *And to her it was granted to be arrayed in fine linen, clean and bright, for the fine linen is the righteous acts of the saints.*
>
> **9** *Then he said to me, "Write: 'Blessed are*

those who are called to the marriage supper of the Lamb!' " And he said to me, "These are the true sayings of God."

We went over how the bride represents the pillar shape that is the heavenly New Jerusalem.

Revelation 21:2 ESV

And I saw the holy city, new Jerusalem, coming down out of heaven from God, prepared as a bride adorned for her husband.

This is the great mystery spoken of in Ephesians 5:32.

Ephesians 5:32 KJV

This is a great mystery: but I speak concerning Christ and the church.

Now if we read Ephesians 5:14 we can verify that we are living in the age of death.

Ephesians 5:14 KJV

14 *Wherefore he saith, Awake thou that sleepest, and arise from the dead, and Christ shall give thee light.*

Once we are born again, our spirits are raised from the spiritual death we have since our birth into this age.

We already went over the fact that the Bible says that Adam would die the day he ate the forbidden fruit. And yet we know his body went on to live hundreds of more years.

This verifies that the Bible was referencing Adam's spirit. His spirit died the day he ate the fruit, and thus opened up the way for death to enter.

Genesis 2:17 KJV

But of the tree of the knowledge of good and evil, thou shalt not eat of it: for in the day that thou eatest thereof thou shalt surely die.

Romans 5:12 KJV

Wherefore, as by one man sin entered into the world, and death by sin; and so death passed upon all men, for that all have sinned:

This is the reason that Jesus Christ had to come in the flesh to this age of death as our Redeemer. To *redeem* means to *buy back*. You cannot *buy back* something you never had in the first place.

Redeem and *ransom* both mean to buy back. *Redeem* is wider in its application than *ransom*, and means to buy back, regain possession of, or exchange for money, goods, etc.

Source: *www.dictionary.com/browse/redeem*

This is also why Jesus is considered the firstborn from this age of death.

The verse that verifies this also verifies His position as the Head of the church - which we know represents a pyramid as the Capstone that we, the Builders, rejected in the previous age.

Colossians 1:18 KJV

And He is the head of the body, the church. He is the beginning, the firstborn from the dead, that in all things He might have the preeminence.

We can get a better understanding of how Jesus Christ and His bride, the church, relates to a husband/wife relationship by reading Ephesians 5:22-33.

Ephesians 5:22-33 KJV

22 *Wives, submit yourselves unto your own husbands, as unto the Lord.*

23 *For the husband is the head of the wife, even as Christ is the head of the church: and he is the saviour of the body.*

24 *Therefore as the church is subject unto Christ, so let the wives be to their own husbands in every thing.*

25 *Husbands, love your wives, even as Christ also loved the church, and gave himself for it;*

26 *That he might sanctify and cleanse it with the washing of water by the word,*

27 *That he might present it to himself a glorious church, not having spot, or wrinkle, or any such thing; but that it should be holy and without blemish.*

28 *So ought men to love their wives as their own bodies. He that loveth his wife loveth himself.*

29 *For no man ever yet hated his own flesh; but nourisheth and cherisheth it, even as the Lord the church:*

30 *For we are members of his body, of his flesh, and of his bones.*

31 *For this cause shall a man leave his*

father and mother, and shall be joined unto his wife, and they two shall be one flesh.

32 *This is a great mystery: but I speak concerning Christ and the church.*

33 *Nevertheless let every one of you in particular so love his wife even as himself; and the wife see that she reverence her husband.*

In verses 31 and 32 it literally says that the two shall become one flesh and that this is a great mystery concerning Christ and the church.

We all, as Christians, make up the body, or pillar, and Christ is the Chief Cornerstone, or Capstone. When you unite the two they become one to form the heavenly New Jerusalem.

This is why we were considered 'gods', with a lower case "g", as the fiancé to Jesus before we rebelled and rejected Him.

Some Christians who don't understand their position as the future bride of Christ have accused me of Mormonism for saying that we were gods.

All this means is that we were beings that were designed to be eternal in the former age that was also designed to be eternal and lit by God's glory.

Jesus was speaking to men when he told them this very thing.

John 10:34 ESV

Jesus answered them, "Is it not written in your Law, 'I said, you are gods'?

Jesus was making reference to Psalm 82:6.

Psalm 82:6 KJV

I have said, Ye are gods; and all of you are children of the most High.

Now if we consider what we already went over, that we were deceived by Lucifer (one of the princes at that time) and we have fallen and been placed under the curse in the age of death where all flesh eventually dies, we see that this is exactly what the very next verse says.

Psalm 82:7 KJV

But ye shall die like men, and fall like one of the princes.

Our fallen spirits enter this age through birth.

I explained, in *The Matrix Code and The Alien Agenda*, how the Elites, or Illuminati (some of which are high ranking leaders in the Catholic church system) know this information because it is passed down to them through fallen angels and Lucifer himself.

They are known to summon up these dark spirits at different gatherings that they hold several times a year.

One of the most widely known gathering locations is *Bohemian Grove.*

Bohemian Grove is a 2,700-acre (1,100 ha) campground located at 20601 Bohemian Avenue, in Monte Rio, California.

This is a perfect example of who our battle is really against.

Ephesians 6:12 HCSB

For our battle is not against flesh and blood, but against the rulers, against the authorities, against the world powers of this darkness, against the spiritual forces of evil in the heavens.

The Elite are aware that we enter this age at birth through the womb. This is why the Catholic Elite worship Mary as the portal over Jesus Christ.

In several instances, Mary is actually a vagina in disguise.

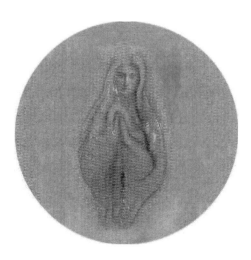

Now we know why Adam was a divine setup. Adam fell right from the beginning to allow everyone, all the fallen, an entryway into this age through birth.

God would never place a perfect, unfallen spirit in a body that has fallen. Adam's flesh, or DNA became corrupt when he ate the fruit and his spirit died the moment he ate the fruit. In no way can Adam pass on a spirit, but he did pass down his fallen and corrupted flesh to all mankind through reproduction.

This is why the Bible says that flesh and blood cannot inherit the kingdom of God. It is because our flesh is corrupt, and this corruption was passed down starting with Adam.

1 Corinthians 15:50 KJV

Now this I say, brethren, that flesh and blood cannot inherit the kingdom of God; neither doth corruption inherit incorruption.

When Adam partook of the forbidden fruit, he was condemned to death. At this time God removed Adam from of a perfect environment located in another dimension here on earth, the Garden of Eden, and placed him in an environment that was literally under the Law - or veil of darkness - that causes the earth to mourn and the heavens above to be black.

This new environment contained entropy which would cause Adam's body to start heading towards decline - or aging - and would eventually lead to his physical death.

The fact that the Law/Torah is the veil of darkness, which in turn is the spoken word of God, has already been proven earlier in this book.

Remember that Hebrews 11:3 gives the location of God's word.

Hebrews 11:3 KJV

Through faith we understand that the worlds were framed by the word of God, so that things which are seen were not made of things which do appear.

So, we know that God's word frames - or surrounds - our universe. This would mean God's word is literally located in the cosmic background.

We also get the exact biblical definition of what God's word or voice sounds like in Ezekiel 43:2.

Ezekiel 43:2 KJV

And, behold, the glory of the God of Israel came from the way of the east: and his voicewas like a noise of many waters: and the earth shined with his glory.

It is not by chance that when we listen to the exact biblical location of God's word, we hear the exact biblical definition of what God's voice sounds like.

If you want to refresh your memory, go to YouTube and type in "Cosmic Background Radiation Ambient Noise."

You can easily compare this to other sources where you can hear a large amount of rushing water.

A good comparison can be found at YouTube by typing in "Niagara Falls Noise Sounds for headache, ADHD, anxiety relief, napping, dreaming."

We already went over the fact that we know God did not start creation under the Law or with a judgment. Therefore, the fact that this Law exists and is stretched over our universe proves that creation did not start with our current earth age.

CHAPTER 8
JESUS AND THE PERFECT LAW

We will use God's word in the literal sense to help us correctly understand further biblical mysteries that have often been misunderstood and the subject of heated debates.

The Bible says that Jesus is the Word of God and that Jesus is God. It also says that all things were made by Him. This is true in the most literal sense.

Since God's ways and thoughts are higher than man's, it is often times hard for man to wrap his mind around the way God chooses to do things. This results in most people placing God in a proverbial box based on what they have been told, taught, or imagine God to be.

If you are not yet convinced that a time gap exists between Genesis 1:1 and 1:2, that's okay because we haven't even scratched the surface yet pertaining to the evidence that confirms this.

Man typically takes the path of least resistance even when making reference to God.

We know the Bible says that God is almighty, omni-present, all knowing, and everlasting, and yet people have trouble believing basic biblical truths because they fall outside of what people observe or think they know about their world.

The fallen angels and Nephilim are a perfect example of this.

Man has invented the Sethite theory because the idea of giants sounds far-fetched based on what we observe today. Once again, we have an example of man trying to interpret the Bible based on his perceptions instead of believing what the Bible literally says through faith and then applying this to what he perceives.

You don't have to follow Steve Quayle or Timothy Alberino for too long before you realize that there is plenty of real, solid, factual evidence proving that giants existed and that this has all been covered up.

Sometimes we forget who the battle is really against.

Ephesians 6:12 KJV

For we wrestle not against flesh and blood, but against principalities, against powers, against the rulers of the darkness of this world, against spiritual wickedness in high places.

Later on in this book you will find out just how literal Ephesians 6:12 is. But for now, I want to show you that the Bible actually says that Jesus is God, Jesus is the Living Word of God, and Jesus is the Perfect Law.

For now, you will have to exercise faith. I will need to show you exactly how our current reality compares to the first and last earth ages to prove scientifically that what the Bible says regarding this is literal fact.

I will do this in later chapters, but I am asking you to take a step of faith and believe what the Bible literally says, regarding the aforementioned issues, at this time.

We will start with what the Bible says about Jesus.

Acts 4:12 KJV

Neither is there salvation in any other: for there is none other name under heaven given among men, whereby we must be saved.

Would you agree that that verse states that

Jesus is the only one that can convert our souls?

Now let's take a look at the Perfect Law.

Psalm 19:7 KJV

The law of the LORD is perfect, converting the soul: the testimony of the LORD is sure, making wise the simple.

Jesus converts our souls. God's Law converts our souls. God's Law is His Word. Jesus is the Living Word of God.

If this is correct, then the second part of Psalm 19:7, *"the testimony of the LORD is sure, making wise the simple"* should also be making reference to Jesus. Jesus should testify to the truth of God's word.

John 18:37 NLT

Pilate said, "So you are a king?" Jesus responded, "You say I am a king. Actually, I was born and came into the world to testify to the truth. All who love the truth recognize that what I say is true."

The Perfect Law and Jesus Christ are one and the same.
We just need to take a look at James 1:23-24 to confirm this.

James 1:23-25 ESV

23 *For if anyone is a hearer of the word and not a doer, he is like a man who looks intently at his natural face in a mirror.*

24 *For he looks at himself and goes away and at once forgets what he was like.*

25 *But the one who looks into the perfect law, the law of liberty, and perseveres, being no hearer who forgets but a doer who acts, he will be blessed in his doing.*

Now let's break it down verse by verse and see what it is actually saying.

23 *For if anyone is a hearer of the word and not a doer, he is like a man who looks intently at his natural face in a mirror.*

"For if anyone is a hearer of the word" - Jesus is the Word - see John 1:1. *"He is like a man who looks intently at his natural face in a mirror."*

As Christians, Jesus lives inside us and we should reflect Jesus. In other words, people should see a reflection of Jesus when they look at us.

24 *For he looks at himself and goes away and at once forgets what he was like.*

What do we look like? We were created in the image of God. We should reflect this image. Jesus and God are one and the same.

John 10:30 KJV

I and my Father are one.

Let's go to verse 25.

25 *But the one who looks into the perfect law, the law of liberty, and perseveres, being no hearer who forgets but a doer who acts, he will be blessed in his doing.*

This confirms that the Perfect Law is Jesus, the same as whom the two previous verses were making reference to. Only Jesus is perfect. Only Jesus liberates us!

John 8:36 KJV

If the Son therefore shall make you free, ye shall be free indeed.

Most don't understand the profound implications behind Jesus and the Perfect Law being one and the same.

This Law, Jesus Christ, appears as a veil of darkness to us from the perspective of man. Would you believe me if I told you that this law actually protects us while giving us the time we have in this life to decide for or against Jesus?

You heard, with your own ears, the sound of vast waters simply by taking God's word literally. These same vast waters act as a protective barrier against the fullness of God's glory.

If the universe was suddenly exposed to all of God's glory at once, it would burn up by the intense heat of the glory of God.

2 Peter 3:10 KJV

But the day of the Lord will come as a thief in the night; in the which the heavens shall pass away with a great noise, and the elements shall melt with fervent heat, the earth also and the works that are therein shall be burned up.

This cosmic layer of water actually comes between us and God's glory which is above the heavens.

Psalm 113:4 KJV

The LORD is high above all nations, and his glory above the heavens.

Job 38:9 describes this veil of darkness as a *"swaddling band"*.

Job 38:9 KJV

When I made the cloud the garment thereof, and thick darkness a swaddling band for it,

Ambrogio Lorenzetti's *Madonna and Child* (1319) depicts swaddling bands.

Swaddling is an age-old practice of wrapping infants in blankets or similar cloths so that movement of the limbs is tightly restricted. Swaddling bands were often used to further restrict the infant.

Some modern medical studies indicate that swaddling helps babies fall asleep and to remain asleep and helps to keep the baby in a supine position which lowers the risk of sudden infant death syndrome (SIDS).

Even Jesus Himself was wrapped in *"swaddling clothes"*.

Luke 2:12 KJV

And this shall be a sign unto you; Ye shall find the babe wrapped in swaddling clothes, lying in a manger.

We need to remember that we are the fallen children of God.

Psalm 82:6-7 KJV

6 *I have said, Ye are gods; and all of you are children of the most High.*

7 *But ye shall die like men, and fall like one of the princes.*

We are fallen, and this fallen universe cannot withstand the fullness of God's glory. God has placed this veil of darkness over our universe to protect us during this age and lifetime while we decide to choose or reject Jesus Christ as Lord and Savior.

So, let's take a close look and see if water can actually act as a shield or barrier.

When it comes to God's glory, it gets a little difficult to come up with any direct comparison and hence it's also difficult to decide just how much protection we would need to shield our fallen universe from the intense heat of His glory.

We can know by God's word that intense heat is one of the effects God's glory would have - and will have - on our fallen world once He removes the barrier between us and His glory/eternity, which is the Torah/Law/Scroll.

Isaiah 34:4 KJV

And all the host of heaven shall be dissolved, and the heavens shall be rolled together as a scroll: and all their host shall fall down, as the leaf falleth off from the vine, and as a falling fig from the fig tree.

The Bible gives a lot of literal clues as to what it is referring to.

In this case the clue is, *"as a scroll."* It is not by chance that the Torah is copied onto a scroll.

At this point, all creation is suddenly exposed to the fullness of God's glory and the result will be everything being burned up by intense heat.

2 Peter 3:10 KJV

But the day of the Lord will come as a thief in

the night; in the which the heavens shall pass away with a great noise, and the elements shall melt with fervent heat, the earth also and the works that are therein shall be burned up.

We know that God's glory clearly outshines the sun, however, the affects must be similar insome ways because the Bible compares the two both in appearance and in the effects. We will start with appearance.

Matthew 17:1-2 KJV

1 *And after six days Jesus taketh Peter, James, and John his brother, and bringeth them up into an high mountain apart,*

2 *And was transfigured before them: and his face did shine as the sun, and his raiment was white as the light.*

So, we can see that appearance of God's glory on Jesus' face is compared to the shining of the sun.

Obviously, the sun is our source of light and heat for our current age and reality. However, when we enter the new age and reality, God's glory will replace the sun as our light.

Isaiah 60:19 KJV

The sun shall be no more thy light by day; neither for brightness shall the moon give light unto thee: but the Lord shall be unto thee an everlasting light, and thy God thy glory.

Since the sun is a small example the Bible gives us to compare to God's glory, we will also use the sun and its gamma rays to test the ability of water to act as a shield or barrier.

This process starts with nuclear fusion at the sun's core and by the time this reaches the sun's surface, it is in the form of gamma rays. One thing that is easy enough to test is the ability of water to shield against nuclear radiation.

According to the following excerpt, water is a very effective radiation shield and as little as seven centimeters of water can cut the radiation level in half.

"We know from the nuclear power industry that spent fuel storage pools are pretty safe places to be around, radiation-wise. They're actually safe to swim in, to a point, because they're serviced routinely by human divers.

They just can't get too close to the spent fuel."

"We use these pools for short-term storage because water is a really good radiation shield. How good?"

"Well, according to a report on the topic prepared for the DoE back in 1977, a layer of water 7 centimeters thick reduces the ionizing radiation (rays and particles) transmitted through it by half (the remainder is captured or moderated to non-ionizing energy levels, mainly heat).

Freshly discharged nuclear fuel puts out about 100,000 R/hour as measured from one foot away in air.

At that rate, certain death is about 5 minutes' exposure and you'd fall into a coma in about 10."

Source:
https://space.stackexchange.com/questions/ 1336/whatthickness-depth-of-water-would- be-required-to-provideradiation-shielding

So, we can see that even a little water is a very effective shield against nuclear radiation.

However, nuclear radiation, or even the sun

itself, can in no way compare to the fullness of God's glory. Therefore, I think it's safe to assume we would need an immense amount of water to act as a barrier or shield between our universe and God's glory.

We know God does not exaggerate and His word says that this barrier is a vast amount of water.

Psalm 29:3 HCSB

The voice of the LORD is above the waters. The God of glory thunders-- the LORD, above vast waters

I think we can safely conclude that a vast amount of water would provide the perfect barrier to protect our fallen universe from the heat and intensity of God's glory.

But we know God's glory is immensely bright and that pure water is largely transparent and yet the Bible describes this veil of water as being dark and black.

Isaiah 50:3 KJV

I clothe the heavens with blackness, and I make sackcloth their covering.

Jeremiah 4:28 KJV

For this shall the earth mourn, and the heavens above be black: because I have spoken it, I have purposed it, and will not repent, neither will I turn back from it.

We also know that the Bible says this is a vast amount of water. So now the question is how much water would it take to completely block out the enormous amount of light that would be given off by God's glory?

Since we can't use God's glory for testing purposes, we will, once again, use the sun.

If you have ever watched a TV show or movie that featured deep sea diving, such as *The Titanic*, then you know that it gets rather dark down in the great depths of the oceans. But how far would one need to go before you reached complete and total darkness? The following excerpt provides the answer.

According to *Water Encyclopedia Science and Issues:*

"The layer of the ocean where no light at all penetrates—over 90 percent of the entire ocean area on Earth—is called the aphotic zone, where depths are more than 1,000 meters (3,300 feet)."

So, we can see that sunlight does not penetrate at all beyond 1,000 meters. As previously mentioned, God's glory is immensely brighter than the sun, but we also know the Bible describes this Torah/veil of water information as being a vast amount of water.

Even a thickness of one-hundred miles would be way less than paper thin when compared to the vastness of our universe.

When we consider the size of the known universe, the odds are in favor of this veil of water being much deeper than a mere one-hundred miles. In any case, God knew exactly what was needed and this veil provides more than enough protection as a shield or barrier, and He obviously created it deep enough to block the light of His glory, leaving this fallen universe in darkness.

CHAPTER 9
THE HOLOGRAPHIC UNIVERSE BY GOD'S DESIGN

Does water provide the necessary components needed to form a hologram?

When one considers the necessary components needed to form a functional hologram, water is probably one of the last things that would come to mind.

A hologram is made by shining a laser onto a partially silvered mirror that is called a beam splitter.

The beam splitter allows part of the laser to pass through the mirror while the reflected part of the laser gets directed to the object that contains the information that will be stored on the holographic plate.

Then both parts of the laser are redirected by other mirrors to meet up again at the holographic plate where the hologram is formed.

You probably noticed that there wasn't any mention of water in that process.

 What we need to keep in mind is that the description you just read is the process used to make a basic holographic still image.

If you wanted to form a projected hologram similar to what can be seen in the original *Star Wars* movie when they were on board the Millennial Falcon playing the holographic life-like game where Han Solo advised C-3PO to "always let the Wookie win". You would need a much more elaborate set-up than what is used to form the typical hologram.

With modern technology, projected, life-like holograms are possible and in recent applications, they are experimenting with water in different forms (liquid, vapor, and even liquid crystals) and getting excellent results.

The following is an excerpt from an article written in 2014 that can be found at *www.engadget.com:*

> "It's 2014 and while we don't have flying cars just yet it looks like interactive holographic displays could be a reality rather soon. The not-so-cleverly-named Leia Display System

(LDS) uses a combination of light, water-vapor and air to provide a transparent canvas for projected images while sensors track movement and touch inputs from users.

The videos we've embedded below show all manner of poking and prodding by users, a bit of *MINORITY REPORT*-style pinching and zooming things in mid-air and even using gestures to rotate and flick stuff out of the way. There's even a sample with a Mercedes sedan driving through the curtain and it "shattering" around the vehicle as it passes through."

An article at *www.nature.com* mentions that they are experimenting with liquid crystals for future 3D holographic movies.

"Holographic technology can produce three-dimensional images that can be seen without special eye-wear and without causing visual fatigue, but the images are usually static.

"Takeo Sasaki and his colleagues at Tokyo University of Science used liquid crystals made from organic compounds to produce a dynamic hologram.

"An electrical field applied to the liquid-crystal mixture alters how this medium bends or refracts, the direction of incoming light.

"The researchers sent coupled laser beams through the crystal mixture to generate a holographic image.

"Although small and monochromatic, the hologram exhibited more than seven times the light amplification of previous attempts and refreshed every 8 milliseconds — fast enough to produce a smooth holographic movie. Such a technique could be used for three-dimensional displays."

So, we see that water and liquid crystals are showing great potential for use in future life-like holographic projections.

By combining crystal chip holographic technology with 3D printers, they are actually making solid physical objects. For now, this technology is still in its infancy and the objects are only paper-clip size.

Here is an excerpt by Jamie Condliffe published on February 17, 2017, from *www.technologyreview.com* explaining this process.

A bright-green laser flashes on, shining into a petri dish full of goo. From nowhere, the shape of a paper clip emerges—ghostly at first, then solid. Five seconds later the clip is fished out, cleaned up, and ready for use.

The basic principle here is an established 3D printing technique that uses lasers to cure a light-activated monomer into solid plastic.

But unlike other approaches, which scan a laser back and forth to create shapes one layer at a time, this system does it all at once using a 3D light field—in other words, a hologram. It could make 3D printing far faster.

At the heart of the device that printed the paper clip is a holographic chip developed by Daqri, a startup that designs and builds augmented-reality devices out of laboratories in San Francisco and in Milton Keynes, U.K. The article goes on to tell how these holograms made from tunable crystals can be projected to assist in forming solid objects.

The advantage of Daqri's chip, the company says, is that it can create holograms without the need for complex optics. On a silicon wafer, a tiny grid of tunable crystals is used to control the magnitude and time delay, or phase, of reflected light shined at the surface of the chip from a laser.

Software adjusts the crystals to create patterns of interference in the light, resulting in a three-dimensional light field. In experiments, the team has used the chip to create solid objects by projecting holograms into containers of various light-activated monomers.

It can currently make small objects, such as a paper clip, in about five seconds—a process that could take a normal 3D printer several minutes to create.

So, we can see that both water and crystals and different combinations of the two are excellent for use in very advanced holographic technologies. I find it interesting that the Bible says that God's throne sits above this firmament of water that surrounds our universe and then in a different scripture reference it mentions the water that is before God's throne is a sea of glass that is like crystal.

Ezekiel 1:26 KJV

And above the firmament that was over their heads was the likeness of a throne, as the appearance of a sapphire stone: and upon the likeness of the throne was the likeness as the appearance of a man above upon it.

Revelation 4:6 KJV

And before the throne there was a sea of glass like unto crystal: and in the midst of the throne, and round about the throne, were four beasts full of eyes before and behind.

CHAPTER 10
CAN WATER STORE VAST AMOUNTS OF INFORMATION?

"The topic of memory in water has fascinated scientists for decades. Computer scientists have tried to understand how water can act in a manner similar to computer chips, potentially storing billions of bits of information in a teaspoon of water."

www.aquatechnology.net

When most people think of water they think of what we use to hydrate our bodies, what we use to wash with, what we use to keep our lawns green, and even to help keep our car engines stay cool. The last thing most people would think of when contemplating the different uses of water would be using it for storing large amounts of information.

Remember, the real question we are asking ourselves is not, 'Do we currently have the technology to use water for storing information?' - but simply, 'Is water capable of storing a large amount of information?'

Modern studies indicate that it is.

There is a difference between having a lot of information and being able to store a lot of information. In order to store and use information, you must have some form of memory. So, the first question we will address will be, 'Does water have memory capabilities?'

The Memory and Secrets of Water - Prof. Dr. Bernd Kröplin

> "When we now see in the drops of water that they talk to another, when information and mental energy seem to generate systematic changes, then it is worthwhile to at least look closer, because this could be the measurable beginning of that which we all know intuitively, that mind permeates matter and that thoughts manifest themselves in material structurings much more extensively than we now think possible.

> "However, memory and information play a significant role in water, and these build a bridge from the immaterial to the material world.

"These subtle phenomena are the ground of misunderstanding, and they can neither be studied nor detected by traditional experimental methods.

"Hence, we use a different approach: we investigate the patterns that appear in a water drop after evaporation of the water and photograph them under a dark field microscope with a magnification between 40 and 400.

"We can prove that the patterns correlate with information exposed to the water.

"For one experiment, the patterns are in most cases so similar that we can speak of reproducibility of the test. The research in bio-resonance lead Prof. Kröplin to the study of water, as the basic element in the body and, hence, the one responsible for transporting much of the information through the different parts of the body at nano, micro, and macro levels.

"Understanding the way water collects and transports information was seen as the essential step to find out the complex behavior of our organs and their reaction to external agents. Water "notes" the external influences that have acted upon it. This is especially important to us humans, as water makes up around 70% of our bodies.

"External factors that we expose ourselves to, be it music, electromagnetic radiation, ultrasound, x-ray or chemical substances, all have an impact on the water structure within our cells that can be seen under a microscope.

"Our research is based on observed phenomena and has a long way still to go."

Prof. Dr. Bernd Kröplin's studies indicate, water has a form of memory, but there is admittedly a long way to go in this research. *P.M Magazine* wrote an article on Dr. Kroplin's research in July of 2005. The following is an excerpt from that article:

"The pattern of the drop pictures," Kröplin is convinced, "are not coincidental." For instance, structures of the drop pictures do change, when water is briefly exposed to the low electromagnetic field of a mobile phone.

"Afterward the microscope pictures show exceptionally clearly visible structures, that are yet limited. "Water has remembered what happened", says Kröplin, "even though the mobile phone had been taken away."

P.M. Magazine – Welt des Wissens Issue July 2005, p. 45-54

Though still in its infancy, the studies indicate that water does have a form of memory. Now the question is, 'Can water be used to store massive amounts of data?

The idea seems logical when we consider that our brains consist of over seventy percent water. This is also an area of research that is still in its infancy, however, it shows great promise and is being pursued by several different research teams.

Ryan Whitwam wrote an article on this research in 2014 that can be found at *www.extremetech.com*. The following is an excerpt from that article, *The Liquid Hard Drive That Could Store a Terabyte of Data in a Tablespoon of Fluid* - by Ryan Whitwam

A team of materials science researchers from the US may have just made the first breakthrough that could make so-called "soft matter" a viable data storage medium — at some incredible storage densities, too.

According to the new research, microscopic particles suspended in liquid could be used to encode the same 1s and 0s stored on solid hard drive platters today. They theorize that clusters of these particles could one day be used to store up to 1TB of data in one tablespoon of liquid hard drive.

Just how much information is in one terabyte?

One terabyte is equal to approximately one thousand gigabytes. This is hard to wrap one's mind around without breaking it down further by applying it to real world situations and seeing what we can get from one gigabyte.

1GB will get you:

- 3,500 emails with a one-word document attachment or

- 5,800 web page views or

- 68 5-minute YouTube videos or

- 230 songs or

- 16 hours of music or

- 1.5 hours of your favorite movie.

This isn't a total number. Each of those tasks would use 1GB by themselves.

However, when you consider that one tablespoon of water can store one thousand gigabytes, it starts to get pretty impressive.

1TB will get you:

- 3,500,000 emails with one word document attachment or

- 5,800,000 web page views or

- 68,000 5-minute YouTube videos or

- 230,000 songs or nearly two years of non-stop music or

- 1,500 hours of your favorite movie.

That's a pretty impressive amount of information for one tablespoon full of water. Now consider how much water it would take to frame our entire universe.

This is in fact what we are talking about with the biblical firmament as it is described in the Bible. Even if this veil of water was one hundred miles deep it would still be far less than paper thin when compared to the immense size of the universe that it surrounds.

If you took all the water from all the oceans on earth, it would not even be equal to one raindrop in the Pacific Ocean on the scale of the amount of water we are talking about here.

The conclusion is that as far as human comprehension is concerned, the amount of information contained in the water of the firmament would basically be infinite.

Now we have established some amazing facts about water.

It happens to be the perfect material that meets all the requirements needed in the Biblical firmament:

1. Water can store vast amounts of information;

2. It has the memory, so it can retain this information;

3. It makes the perfect protective shield or barrier;

4. It provides all the necessary components needed to form a very high-tech hologram except for the actual laser itself.

God's glory takes the place of the laser to illuminate and project the information in the veil of water that frames our universe. God allowed a small beam of His glory in the form of what we would call the theoretical white-hole to enter our reality the moment He said, *"Let there be light."*

We need to ask ourselves what the odds are that the Bible describes a firmament of water encompassing our universe and that water just happens to meet all the needed, and very extreme requirements in order to fulfill all of the individual and very specific tasks?

The Bible describes Jesus as the Word, God as Light, and the Holy Spirit as Living Water. The Bible also describes the Three as One and forming the Holy Trinity.

All three work together to form our reality.

The Torah is the Word of God that frames our universe.

The Water is the material that the Torah is made from and it holds and stores the information. The Light is the Glory of God that illuminates and projects the information. All three become one to form our universe. The Bible says that God made the heavens and the earth, but in other passages, it describes teamwork and goes on to say that the team was one.

Genesis 1:1 KJV

In the beginning God created the heaven and the earth.

John 1:1 KJV

In the beginning was the Word, and the Word was with God, and the Word was God.

Jesus is the Word mentioned in John 1:1.

God is Light as mentioned in 1 John 1:5

1 John 1:5 KJV

This then is the message which we have heard of him, and declare unto you, that God is light, and in him is no darkness at all.

The Holy Spirit is Living Water as mentioned in John 7:37-39

John 7:37-39 KJV

37 *In the last day, that great day of the feast, Jesus stood and cried, saying, If any man thirst, let him come unto me, and drink.*

38 *He that believeth on me, as the scripture hath said, out of his belly shall flow rivers of living water.*

39 *(But this spake he of the Spirit, which they that believe on him should receive: for the Holy Ghost was not yet given; because that Jesus was not yet glorified.)*

All this information may seem like a stretch, especially for those who are not familiar with quantum physics, or who have had a different perception of how all this works which they have believed and held on to for years.

I can certainly understand that, but I assure you that everything we have covered will be proven beyond any doubt at the conclusion of this book to anyone who is willing to weigh out the overwhelming evidence presented, especially when compared to the theories and conjecture that they have been conditioned to believe to be true through many outlets such as public school systems and mainstream media.

In the next chapter. we will talk about how all this information would come together to form our reality and universe based on God's word and scientific analysis.

CHAPTER 11
EXPLAINING REALITY

"Imagine that everything you see, feel and hear in three dimensions, and your perception of time, in fact emanates from a flat two-dimensional field." -Professor Kostas Skenderis, University of Southampton

While theories of holographic universes have been around since the 1990s, the latest study published in the journal *Physical Review Letters* contains the first proof. The researchers say:

"'We are proposing using this holographic Universe, which is a very different model of the Big Bang than the popularly accepted one that relies on gravity and inflation,' said Niayesh Afshordi, from the University of Waterloo and Perimeter Institute, and lead author of the study.

"'Each of these models makes distinct predictions that we can test as we refine our data and improve our theoretical understanding, all within the next five years,'

Afshordi said. 'Holography is a huge leap

forward in the way we think about the structure and creation of the Universe,' added Skenderis."

Source: *http://www.wired.co.uk/article/ouruniverse-is-a-hologram*

Would you believe it if I told you they came to this conclusion by studying the Cosmic Background?

Similarly, in 1982 a landmark experiment performed by a research team led by physicist Alain Aspect at the Institute of Theoretical and Applied Optics in Paris demonstrated that the web of subatomic particles that compose our physical universe - the very fabric of reality itself - possesses what appears to be an undeniable "holographic" property.

Theoretical physicist Dr. James Gates, Jr. discovered binary code at the quantum level. We are talking about quantum bits of 1's and 0's. The idea that we live in a holographic universe that uses a form of quantum "computer code" to create the physical reality is not a new idea.

In the 1940s, some physicists suggested that we live in a "computer generated" universe.

Physicists James Gates talks about this form of computer code which he refers to as *"adinkras"* in the YouTube video titled *"Theoretical Physicist Finds Computer Code in String Theory"*.

The core structures of reality work similar to how a computer works. A computer communicates and operates through the use of binary codes, which are codes that consist of ones (on) and zeros (off). Binary codes are very simple, but with the right combinations, they can help computers create magnificent things.

For example, when we paint a picture using a computer software, the core state of the colors and shapes in the picture are basically made of ones and zeros.

We do not see our picture as ones and zeros because the central processing unit (CPU) and its counterparts process the binary codes as colors and shapes. The greatest thing about binary codes is that there are no limits to their combinations.

The simple process of using binary codes to create things within the hardware of computers is very similar to how Creation creates our external reality or material world.

The material world works very similar to a virtual reality. At its core, the material world is made of only light (energy) that flashes on and off to create energy codes.

The idea that we live in a holographic universe is very real. With the invention of quantum computers, physicists should soon be able to prove this beyond a reasonable doubt.

So, what does it mean that we live in a holographic universe generated by some kind of quantum computer? It means that the Universe was created by an intelligent creator, and therefore it was not created by accident. In other words, the Prime Creator exists!

Source: *https://www.sott.net/article/301611-Livingin-the-Matrix-Physicist-finds-computer-codeembedded-in-string-theory*

"Examples of fractals are everywhere in nature. They can be found in the patterns of trees, branches, and ferns, in which each part appears to be a smaller image of the whole.

"They are found in the branch-like patterns of river systems, lightning, and blood vessels. They can be seen in snowflakes, seashells, crystals, and mountain ranges. We can even see the holographic and fractal-like nature of reality in the structure of the Universe itself, as the clusters of galaxies and dark matter resemble the neurons in our brain, the mycelium network of fungi, as well as the network of the man-made Internet." -Joseph P. Kauffman

The late Michael Talbot published the book *The Holographic Universe* in 1991. Michael had this to say;

"Put it another way, there is evidence to suggest that our world and everything in it- from snowflakes to maple trees to falling stars and spinning electrons-are also only ghostly images, projections from a level of reality so beyond our own it is literally beyond both space and time."

The Bible describes a veil consisting of a vast amount of water that is surrounding our universe.

Light cannot penetrate this veil, and hence, this veil would be black and leave our universe encased in darkness.

Isaiah 50:3 KJV

I clothe the heavens with blackness, and I

make sackcloth their covering.

This water that forms the veil of darkness is not still - like a pond - but is actually rushing water like you would find in a fast-flowing river. You can verify this when you listen to cosmic background noise. Still water is silent, but you can hear rushing water.

Genesis 1:6-7 NLT

6 *Then God said, "Let there be a space between the waters, to separate the waters of the heavens from the waters of the earth."*

7 *And that is what happened.*

God made this space to separate the waters of the earth from the waters of the heavens.

When one realizes that the *"waters of the heavens"* is actually making reference to the veil of darkness that frames our universe, and that the *"space between"* is what we know as outer-space, and then the other reference point is the *"waters of the earth",* we understand that what we have here is biblical verification of the Planck satellite finding: the earth is truly at the center of the universe.

We will cover the Planck satellite findings in detail in the next chapter.

Water can also act as the beam splitter or partially silvered mirror used to form a hologram. By observing how water interacts with the rays of light from the sun we can see that it absorbs part of the light and reflects part of it.

The water that forms the veil that surrounds our universe also contains the massive amount of information that is needed.

Unlike a typical hologram where the beam splitting mirror and the information, or object, are two separate things, with the high-tech hologram that forms our reality, the beam splitter and the information are one and the same in the form of rushing water.

However, unlike the typical rushing water that almost seems chaotic, this rushing water has every part at every moment intricately guided by God.

God is awesome beyond the imagination of man according to the Bible.

What I find interesting is that one of the passages that mentions this also compares it to the heavens being higher than the earth.

Isaiah 55:8-9 KJV

8 *For my thoughts are not your thoughts, neither are your ways my ways, saith the Lord.*

9 *For as the heavens are higher than the earth, so are my ways higher than your ways, and my thoughts than your thoughts.*

I think it's safe to say that man will never completely comprehend the things of God in this lifetime, but we can apply what we have learned in His word to what we know about holograms, and holographic projection, and get an idea of how creation works by God's design.

When God said, *"Let there be light",* there was a sudden explosion of light that most people think of as the Big Bang.

Light was not created at that moment. God simply opened a portal from eternity and let a sliver of His glory shine in. We can be certain of this because God is light, and eternity is filled with His glory. Therefore, light has always existed. Eternity that is beyond our universe or *"above the heavens"* is lit by God's glory.

Psalm 8:1 KJV

O LORD our Lord, how excellent is thy name

in all the earth! who hast set thy glory above the heavens.

The scientific definition for this explosion of light would be the theoretical white-hole.

The biblical and scientific information indicates that this is likely located at the center of our Milky Way galaxy. We will also cover this in the next chapter.

In the typical hologram, the beam splitter or partially silvered mirror is separate from the information or object used to form the hologram. Of course, a hologram that forms our reality is anything but typical. Let's try and get a picture in our minds of what we are searching for.

We know the information, or Law/Torah is described in the Bible as a veil that frames or surrounds our universe. This would likely be spherical because it frames our universe.

The Bible says that our universe is finite and describes it as a cloth that will be rolled up by Jesus at the end of this age.

Isaiah 50:3 KJV

I clothe the heavens with blackness, and I make sackcloth their covering.

The Bible also describes the earth as waxing old like a garment and the heavens vanishing like smoke. When Jesus removes the veil that, is the information that forms our holographic reality.

Isaiah 51:6 KJV

Lift up your eyes to the heavens, and look upon the earth beneath: for the heavens shall vanish away like smoke, and the earth shall wax old like a garment, and they that dwell therein shall die in like manner: but my salvation shall be for ever, and my righteousness shall not be abolished.

If the universe is infinite, modern science gives it a different shape. However, if the universe is finite, modern science suggests it would take on the form of a sphere.

The following are excerpts *from https://www.space.com/24309-shape-of-theuniverse.html*

If you could somehow manage to step outside of the universe, what would it look like? Scientists have struggled with this question, taking several different measurements in order to determine the geometry of the cosmos and whether or not it will come to an end.

How do they measure the shape of the universe? And what have they found?

The shape of the universe depends on its density. If the density is more than the critical density, the universe is closed and curves like a sphere; if less, it will curve like a saddle. But if the actual density of the universe is equal to the critical density, as scientists think it is, then it will extend forever like a flat piece of paper.

Credit: *NASA/WMAP Science team:*

If the actual density of the universe is greater than the critical density, then it contains enough mass to eventually stop its expansion.

In this case, the universe is closed and finite, though it has no end, and has a spherical shape.

Once the universe stops expanding, it will begin to contract. Galaxies will stop receding and start moving closer and closer together. Eventually, the universe will undergo the opposite of the Big Bang, often called the

"Big Crunch." This is known as a closed universe.

Those excerpts shown from *www.space.com* admit that in a closed or finite universe the shape would be spherical.

They also say that they don't believe this is the case because they think the universe is eternal and hence the shape would be something other than spherical.

As Christians we know God's word is absolute truth and therefore we know the universe is finite in both space and time, in which case both the Bible and modern science would show the universe being spherical.

So, if we could see the universe or Torah/Law as an observer from the outside, it would likely look something like the depiction given in the following drawing:

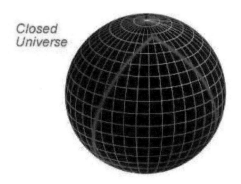

Closed Universe

Keep in mind that what you are looking at would be the information that surrounds our universe, or the veil of darkness, and our reality would then be a projection of this that would end up in the center of this projected information. So, I will give a cutaway depiction to get a better idea of what we are talking about. The black sphere in the center of the cutaway drawing would represent our reality or universe:

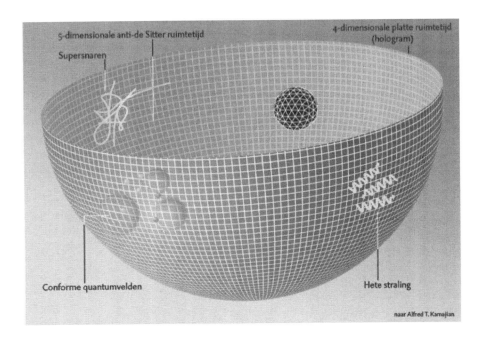

naar Alfred T. Kamajian

The veil of water that encircles our universe would absorb part of this light and reflect part, allowing the light to interact and merge with the information/water and at the same time be projected towards the center of the spherical veil where everything would intersect to form our holographic reality.

This action would keep repeating as the light continued to reflect from different areas of the inside of the spherical veil of darkness.

Since the water is flowing it would constantly be redirecting massive amounts of information into the hologram causing it to form our living reality as we perceive it.

To say that I have over-simplified this explanation would be a very drastic understatement. But it does give us a basic idea of how it works that we can all wrap our minds around.

If you had God's view from eternity and were looking down on this veil of darkness that is made of water and surrounds our spherical shaped universe, it could possibly look something like the photo on the following page.

The Bible says that God spoke the universe into existence.

When we speak, the sound is made of vibrations at different frequencies that come from our vocal cords.

So, one would think that creation would contain these frequencies and vibrations that would be caused by the voice of God speaking the Hebrew Torah.

"If you want to find the secrets of the universe, think in terms of energy, frequency and vibration." -Nikola Tesla

If God used an audible voice during creation, then one would think that we would somehow be able to hear God's voice within creation. This is, in fact, what you are hearing when you listen to the cosmic background.

Psalm 19:1 KJV

The heavens declare the glory of God; and the firmament sheweth his handywork.

Jesus Christ is literally the foundation of all reality.

Colossians 1:17 KJV

And he is before all things, and by him all things consist.

Now, remember, the very next verse gives the shape that represents Jesus Christ as the quantum foundational building block that comes before all reality and holds all reality together, which is a pyramid shape.

Colossians 1:18 KJV

And he is the head of the body, the church:

who is the beginning, the firstborn from the dead; that in all things he might have the preeminence.

This is a perfect example of how we can start with God's word and compare it to scientific studies.

The description of New Jerusalem states that *"the city lieth foursquare, and the length is as large as the breadth: and he measured the city with the reed, twelve thousand furlongs. The length and the breadth and the height of it are equal."*

The key to understanding the true shape lays within the details of the description in context.

"The city LIETH foursquare." It is making reference to the base or the part that *"lays"* on the ground. A pyramid "lieth" foursquare, but a cube is squared regardless of if you are talking about the top, side or bottom.

A pyramid is also the same length, width, and height in keeping with the measurements given

in scripture. Keep in mind that Christ is the chief head stone that the builders rejected.

Matthew 21:42 KJV

Jesus saith unto them, Did ye never read in

the scriptures, The stone which the builders rejected, the same is become the head of the corner: this is the Lord's doing, and it is marvellous in our eyes?

Psalm 118:22 AKJV

The stone which the builders refused is become the head stone of the corner.

Mark 12:10 KJV

And have ye not read this scripture; The stone which the builders rejected is become the head of the corner:

We know that *"head"* makes reference to the top or capstone, and we know that all four corners of a pyramid meet at the head or capstone, making the capstone the head of the corners.

We know the New Jerusalem represents the Bride and body of Christ which is the church.

Jesus is the Head of the church, or Headstone, which would be the shape of a pyramid.

Once we understand the shape that represents Jesus Christ, we can unlock verses that reveal the secrets of quantum physics.

For example, recent studies in quantum physics

indicate that the smallest shape in our reality is a pyramid. We know this represents Jesus Christ who is the Head of the church. A Planck Length is the smallest division of matter at the quantum level, and the first shape it will end up forming is a tetrahedron.

In other words, the pyramid shape comes before all other physical matter and is the "building block" that all physical matter starts with. With that in mind, let's take a look at quantum physics in the Bible.

Colossians 1:16-20 KJV

16 *For by him were all things created, that are in heaven, and that are in earth, visible and invisible, whether they be thrones, or dominions, or principalities, or powers: all things were created by him, and for him:*

17 *And he is before all things, and by him all things consist.*

18 *And he is the head of the body, the church: who is the beginning, the firstborn from the dead; that in all things he might have the preeminence.*

Christ is before all things (the Planck Length comes before all other matter), and then it goes on to give the pyramid shape when it states that Christ is the Head (pyramid shaped capstone) of the body (the New Jerusalem or church) who is the beginning.

I realize we touched on this information earlier, but it is important to remind you so that you can see how this is confirmed in amazing ways.

Our reality is temporary, and passing away, according to the Bible, and Jesus Christ is eternal. Everything in our reality is just a dim mirror reflection of eternity.

1 Corinthians 13:12 NLT

Now we see things imperfectly, like puzzling reflections in a mirror, but then we will see everything with perfect clarity. All that I know now is partial and incomplete, but then I will know everything completely, just as God now knows me completely.

This means that the tetrahedron is just a temporary mirror reflection of the eternal makeup of Jesus Christ. As 1 Corinthians 13:12 states, what we see in this reality is partial and incomplete.

The tetrahedron is partial and incomplete. It is missing the fourth side at the base.

The base of a tetrahedron only has three sides and the eternal headstone shape that represents Jesus Christ has a four-sided base, yet both are pyramids.

When you look in the mirror you cannot see the bottom of your feet. When you look at a tetrahedron in the mirror you cannot see beneath it, or its base. You can only see the face, which is a triangle.

When you look at the face of the pyramid shape that represents Jesus Christ in a mirror, you will see the same exact shape, a triangle.

This is where things get really interesting. If you combine two tetrahedrons at the quantum level, you get what we could refer to as the first quantum building block beyond the pyramid shape in our reality.

When you connect all the outside points you get a hexagon.

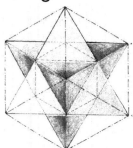

A hexagon has six sides and we can see it in natural formations such as the honeycomb in a beehive. There is strong evidence supporting this as one of the foundational building blocks of our reality.

It's as if the inner atomic structure of gas giant planets is projected to the poles. If we take a look at the poles on Saturn and Neptune, we will find the hexagon shape.

Infrared instruments see Saturn by the thermal radiation emitted from its interior, and they have been getting fantastic views of the hexagon.

The following is a photo of Saturn's north pole that was originally discovered during the Voyager flybys of Saturn in the 1980s.

The number 6 refers to earthly matters, and you can find naturally occurring instances of 6 in magnified photos of water crystals and snowflakes. Slice open a tomato or bell pepper and you often find six chambers. Honeycombs are shaped as 6-sided hexagons.

In the Bible, the number 6 symbolizes man and human weakness, the evils of Satan, and the manifestation of sin. Man was created on the sixth day. Men are appointed 6 days to labor.

The sixth commandment prohibits the murder of man and represents the unholy trinity of the beast, and his number is 666. This is why it is sometimes referred to as an unholy trinity, and as such, the bringing together of three 6's is the number and mark of the end time Beast of Revelation.

Revelation 13:18 NLT

Wisdom is needed here. Let the one with understanding solve the meaning of the number of the beast, for it is the number of a man. His number is 666.

So, we can see that the number 6 prevails in this temporarily fallen universe that we live in and 666 is the number of the beast, or

Antichrist, who is Satan in the flesh. This is just another example of Satan putting his evil twist on something God has done in order to try and replicate Jesus Christ, and thereby deceive mankind.

Let's do a quick review.

The tetrahedron is a pyramid with a three-sided base that is a mirror image of Jesus Christ who represents the pyramid shape with a four-sided base, which is a quadrilateral pyramid.

The first quantum building block we get by combining two tetrahedrons has six points and is hexagonal. Jesus comes before all reality and holds all reality together.

Colossians 1:17 ESV

And he is before all things, and in him all things hold together.

The hexagon is derived from the tetrahedron and is just the mirror image of Christ. It represents a temporary reality that is passing away and fallen.

It also represents 6, the number of man. Man was created in the image of God.

Genesis 1:27 KJV

So God created man in his own image, in the image of God created he him; male and female created he them.

If we wanted an exact representation of Jesus Christ as the Head Stone or the Head of the church, we would get a pyramid with a four-sided base, or a quadrilateral pyramid.

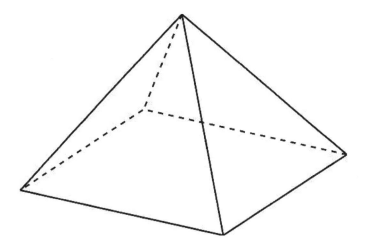

If we combine two quadrilateral pyramids we will get the first quantum building block for an eternal reality.
It has eight sides. If you connect the edges you will get an octagon.

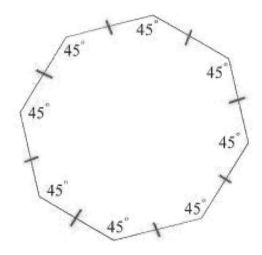

The octagon stands for:

Regeneration

Totality

Infinity

Rebirth

We are regenerated through Jesus Christ.

2 Corinthians 5:17 KJV

Therefore if any man be in Christ, he is a new creature: old things are passed away; behold, all things are become new.

Jesus Christ is the totality of all existence.

Colossians 1:17 ESV

And he is before all things, and in him all things hold together.

Jesus is infinite.

Revelation 1:8 KJV

I am Alpha and Omega, the beginning and the ending, saith the Lord, which is, and which was, and which is to come, the Almighty.

Jesus gives us spiritual Rebirth.

John 3:3 KJV

Jesus answered and said unto him, Verily, verily, I say unto thee, Except a man be born again, he cannot see the kingdom of God.

Interestingly, the two overlapping squares form what is known as the Seal, or Signet of Melchizedek.

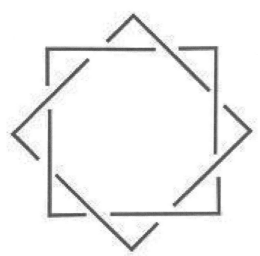

The Signet of Melchizedek

"The Signet of Melchizedek, King of Righteousness and Priest of the Most High God; King of Schalaam, which is King of Peace - the Octalpha or eightfold endless triangle, which, being a geometric figure composed of lines continually reproduced to infinity, by right angles, horizontals, perpendiculars and diagonals, was hailed by our ancient brethern among all nations, as the symbol of the Divine Omnipotence, Omniscience and Omnipresence; universal, infinite and eternal."

This seal has been taken over and abused by several pagan religions, but Melchizedek was mentioned in Psalm 110:1- 4 as an example of Jesus Christ being our priest forever.

Psalm 110:1- 4 KJV

1 *The Lord said unto my Lord, Sit thou at my right hand, until I make thine enemies thy footstool.*

2 *The Lord shall send the rod of thy strength out of Zion: rule thou in the midst of thine enemies.*

3 *Thy people shall be willing in the day of thy power, in the beauties of holiness from the womb of the morning: thou hast the dew of thy youth.*

4 *The Lord hath sworn, and will not repent, Thou art a priest for ever after the order of Melchizedek.*

The octagon has eight sides and the number of Jesus is 888!

Using the Greek Ionic Ciphered Numeral System scientifically proves this. In this system, each letter of the Greek alphabet is assigned a numerical value. The name of Jesus in Greek is spelled *I H S O U S (iota, eta, sigma, omicron, upsilon, sigma).*

Substituting in the Greek numeral system the equivalent numerical values to each letter in the name of Jesus and adding them up, the total is 888. The values of each letter are: *iota,* 10; *eta,* 8; *sigma,* 200; *omicron,* 70; *upsilon,* 400; *sigma,* 200. The sum of 10 + 8 + 200 + 70 + 400 + 200 is 888.

Now we can understand why the tetrahedron is an incomplete and temporary mirror reflection representing our current reality and the eternal pyramid shape with a square base represents Jesus Christ at the quantum level of an eternal reality.

If you are a doubter and think this is scripture

out of context, I can prove this point as it is verified throughout the Bible.

We know the Bible says Jesus is the Word and we just went quantum showing that Jesus is *"the beginning."*

He is *"before all things, and by him all things consist."* Jesus represents the first shape or building block in our reality after the Planck Length, which is a tetrahedron or pyramid (head; capstone) when we are at the quantum level.

Let's give another example.

John 1-4 (KJV)

1 *In the beginning was the Word, and the Word was with God, and the Word was God.*

2 *The same was in the beginning with God.*

3 *All things were made by him; and without him was not any thing made that was made.*

4 *In him was life; and the life was the light of men.*

Not only does John 1-4 repeat what we just verified in Colossians 1:16-20, but it goes on to say, *"In him was life; and the life was the light of men."*

Starting with the Planck Length, everything in the universe starts with, is held together by, and consists of light.

Light is literally what forms and gives life at the quantum level.

Our universe started with a sudden explosion of light.

Genesis 1:3 KJV

And God said, Let there be light: and there was light.

CHAPTER 12
THE TORAH

(THE QUANTUM SOURCE CODE)

Could the Torah actually be the source code at the quantum level that generates our reality?

Research on quantum physics indicates we are living in a holographic universe, and there is solid science to support this hypothesis. It took a mind like Albert Einstein's to see the truth in this years ago when he said: "Reality is merely an illusion, albeit a very persistent one".

As modern science advances, will it finally prove the Bible wrong? Or is it possible that quantum physics and even the holographic universe are somehow biblical?

In the realization that not everyone studies quantum physics, I will do my best to present all of the findings and information in layman's terms that will be easy for everyone to follow.

Let's start by defining quantum mechanics or quantum physics. According to *Wikipedia* the definition of quantum mechanics is as follows:

> "Quantum mechanics is the science of the very small: the body of scientific principles that explains the behavior of matter and its interactions with energy on the scale of atoms and subatomic particles."

To keep it simple, according to quantum physics, all matter is made of energy vibrations at different frequencies. The positive and negative charges in these energy/atoms make it attract or repel to give it the different states and densities that we recognize as the physical matter that we relate to.

So, we have the illusion of solid physical matter in a universe made up of energy vibrations or in other words, a digital universe.

> "If you want to find the secrets of the Universe, think in terms of energy, frequency, and vibration." -Nikola Tesla

The holographic universe principle says that mathematically all the information in our 3D universe can be encoded or written on a 2D surface. In other words, our reality is a holographic projection of the information on a 2D surface.

There is pretty solid data (no pun intended) to back up this theory. However, there are several that go beyond the solid data and hypothesize that we all have what they call an infinite "I" that is in this holographic field of Infinite possibilities.

They claim that we can each tap into our infinite "I" to help mold and shape our future. In my opinion, at this point, they have left solid science and entered the world of pure conjecture.

Before we go any further, let's define "Hologram".

According to Merriam-Webster dictionary, a hologram is a three-dimensional image reproduced from a pattern of interference produced by a split coherent beam of radiation (as a laser).

Whatis.com describes a hologram as a three-dimensional image, created with photographic projection. The term is taken from the Greek words *holos* (whole) and *gramma* (message).

I find it interesting that the root words of hologram literally means *Whole Message*.

I want the reader to keep in mind that Christians view the Bible as God's whole message to mankind.

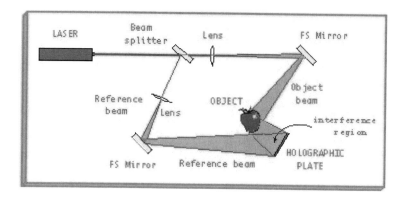

Now that we have the definition of hologram let's try to define the principles behind the theory of the holographic universe.

Wikipedia gives a lengthy definition of the holographic principle, but I think it will be worth your time in order to get a better understanding of the holographic universe.

The holographic principle is a property of string theories and a supposed property of quantum gravity that states that the description of a volume of space can be thought of as encoded on a boundary to the region—preferably a light-like boundary like a gravitational horizon.

First proposed by Gerard 't Hooft, it was given a precise string theory interpretation by Leonard

Susskind who combined his ideas with previous ones of 't Hooft and Charles Thorn.

As pointed out by Raphael Bousso, Thorn observed in 1978 that string theory admits a lower dimensional description in which gravity emerges from it in what would now be called a holographic way.

In a larger sense, the theory suggests that the entire universe can be seen as two-dimensional information on the cosmological horizon, the event horizon from which information may still be gathered and not lost due to the natural limitations of space-time supporting a black hole, an observer, and a given setting of these specific elements, *[clarification needed]* such that the three dimensions we observe are an effective description only at macroscopic scales and at low energies.

Cosmological holography has not been made mathematically precise, partly because the particle horizon has a non-zero area and grows with time.

The holographic principle was inspired by black hole thermodynamics which conjectures that the maximal entropy in any region scales with the radius squared, and not cubed as might be expected.

In the case of a black hole, the insight was that the informational content of all the objects that have fallen into the hole might be entirely contained in surface fluctuations of the event horizon.

The holographic principle resolves the black hole information paradox within the framework of string theory.

However, there exists classical solutions to the Einstein equations that allow values of the entropy larger than those allowed by an area law, hence in principle, larger than those of a black hole.

I would like to note that the first step in making a hologram is taking a source of light (a laser) and projecting it onto a partially silvered mirror called a beam splitter.

I find it interesting that the Bible says:

1 John 1:5

"This is the message we have heard from Him and announce to you, that God is Light, and in Him there is no darkness at all."

And Paul compares our physical reality as Christians to eternity with the Lord by using a dim mirror, or one could say, a partially silvered mirror.

1 Corinthians 13:12

"For now we see in a mirror, dimly, but then face to face. Now I know in part, but then I shall know just as I also am known."

So, one could say that our reality is only a dim reflection of eternity.

As previously stated, before the fall of Satan the only light the universe needed was the Light of God. However, after Satan's Fall, God placed the universe under a veil of darkness.

Isaiah 50:3

"I clothe the heavens with blackness, and I make sackcloth their covering."

Before the fall of Satan, the light of the universe was the Glory of God.

So, when Satan made the statement found in

Isaiah 14:13:

"I will ascend into heaven, I will exalt my throne above the stars of God: I will sit also

upon the mount of the congregation, in the sides of the north"

It was right before Satan's fall and therefore right before God placed the veil of darkness over the universe.

This clearly goes against the argument that heaven is in our universe.

Heaven is to the North beyond the veil of darkness. The veil covers the cursed universe we live in during this current earth age, and as previously stated, it will be removed after this age.

Man's mind cannot comprehend eternity outside the veil. However, there are many deep mysteries that lay beneath the veil in the reality we perceive.

I believe God has put these mysteries here for us to observe, study, and hopefully solve. The deep mystery we are trying to solve now is simply, 'Does the Bible support the idea of a holographic universe?'

(If you consider the fact that it is only our current age that is holographic and formed by the Torah/Law - or veil of darkness - and that the first and final age were not holographic, because those realities were - and will be - lit by God's glory and will be eternal - not generated by the Torah. You can see why it is important to understand the different realities when discussing the different earth ages.)

The answer to this question is so amazing that odds are you will never look at the universe around you or how you perceive your reality the same again after you finish reading about this.

First, we will investigate the plain text of the Bible to see if there is any information that would support or lead us to believe that our universe could be a hologram.

A Biblical Analogy by Chuck Missler

"When one examines a hologram in natural (uncollimated, noncoherent) light, it has no apparent form nor attractiveness.

"However, when one examines it with the laser with which it was formulated, a three-dimensional image appears.

"When one examines the Bible in unaided, natural light, it *'has no form nor comeliness that we should desire it.'*

"But when we examine it illuminated by the Light that created it, the Spirit of God that put it all together in the first place, we see an image: the image of the One that every detail in it illuminates, the promised Messiah Himself."

Source: *http://www.khouse.org*

Most of us are aware that the Bible mentioned spirits in several cases, such as Angels and Demons. It is also well known that spirits seem to have the ability to pass through solid physical matter unaffected.

This seems to indicate that they are not part of our reality or our holographic projection.

Let's say our reality resembles a holodeck. If you are part of the holodeck you can interact with others in the holodeck (the physical world as we know it, the illusion). If you are outside the holodeck, you will simply pass through the holodeck as if walking through a holographic projection.

This explains why the real world (the spiritual) can easily pass through what we perceive as reality - which is actually more of an illusionary world.

For example, let's say we have three guys, one is in London, England, and the other two are in

New York.

The man in London is on a stage that is set up to receive a live holographic image. Likewise, the two guys in New York have the ability to project their holographic image onto the stage of the man in London. So, they do just that.

The guy in London can talk and interact with them and see them in 3D as if they were actually there. Yet, if he goes to touch them he will just pass right through them. However, the two guys projected in the hologram have no problem touching each other as solid objects.

This is exactly what we observed when we see a spirit. So, what if the reality that we perceive as being real is actually only a holographic projection - a vague and dimly lit reflection of the truly real reality which is eternity which lies beyond the veil.

Could this be what Paul is saying in 1 Corinthians 13:12?

1 Corinthians 13:12 ESV

For now we see in a mirror dimly, but then face to face. Now I know in part; then I shall know fully, even as I have been fully known.

Genesis 1:27

So God created mankind in his own image, in the image of God he created them; male and female he created them.

Duality placed in the image - made from nothing.

Hebrews 11:3

By faith we understand that the universe was formed at God's command, so that what is seen was not made out of what was visible.

As the theory suggests, the hologram itself is not visible apart from the light shined on the image. Faith is the ability of the observer to collapse the wave function.

A perfect description of this is found in John 1. *Word* is information. *Light* reveals what it hits. The key here is to see light as the engagement of the interference pattern.

John 1:1-5

1 *In the beginning was the Word, and the Word was with God, and the Word was God.*

2 *He was with God in the beginning.*

3 *Through him all things were made; without him nothing was made that has been made.*

4 *In him was life, and that life was the light of all mankind.*

5 *The light shines in the darkness, and the darkness has not overcome it.*

There is evidence that our universe is not analog, but digital.

So, we can see that the Bible in plain text does seem to hint at the possibility that we live in a holographic universe.

Now, this is where things get really interesting.

Isaac Newton spent most of his life searching for a code in the Bible. I believe it was largely due to the lack of computer technology in his day that he was unsuccessful in his pursuit. However, he did have this to say;

> "The entire universe is a cryptogram set by the Almighty." -Sir Isaac Newton

Years later, after the invention of the computer, it was discovered that by dividing up the letters of the Torah into skip sequences, one could find words and sentences with significant meaning that had been encoded. We know this as the Torah codes.

The following statement can be found at *www.endtodarkness.com:*

"There is a code in the Torah, the first five books of the Old Testament. The Code is real and mathematically provable.

"Incredibly, the Code seems to have information about what has happened in the past and is happening today. Names, places, and events are all encoded.

"The Torah is not a crystal ball but new clues seem to indicate that it was meant for our generation to discover its secrets.

"Since the first introduction of computers in the 70s, a select group of rabbis and professors have been working to crack the Code.

"In this movie, *Torah Codes: End to Darkness*, we interview them and uncover what they have discovered."

Several verses and passages in the Bible have an obvious meaning that we get from reading the plain text, but they also have a dual meaning - or an underlying meaning.

An example of this is the king of Tyre which also makes reference to Satan in Ezekial 28. See *https://www.gotquestions.org/King-of-Tyre.html* for more info on this.

Could 2 Timothy 2:15 be another example of this?

2 Timothy 2:15 KJV

Study to shew thyself approved unto God, a workman that needeth not to be ashamed, rightly dividing the word of truth.

The *Word of Truth* (the Bible, or more specifically, the Torah codes) when divided correctly, gives us the encoded information.

People who have studied and tested the Bible code have some interesting things to say about it.

"Every major event in world history, every major figure in world history, seems to be encoded in the Bible." -Michael Drosnin

"The Bible codes are a dramatic demonstration that what we have here really is the word of God and not simply a historical tradition.

These 66 books penned by 40 different guys over thousands of years are collectively a supernaturally given, and skillfully engineered, message system." -Chuck Missler

Ordinarily we would assume that the US Pentagon and anything having to do with the Bible would be far removed from one another.

But in 1994 statistical science, a respected mathematical Journal published report number three, volume 9 titled *"Equal Distant Letter Sequences in the Book of Genesis"*.

That report found its way to the Pentagon's national secret agency of cryptology and made it to the desk of Harold Gans, a senior cryptographer for the Pentagon's National Security Agency.

Gans knew that equal letter Skip sequence was a code form widely used by governments and their agents.

The idea that they would occur in the book of Genesis was hard for him to believe. He found it so difficult to believe that he wrote his own computer program based on his intimate knowledge of encryption techniques with the intent of disproving the results published by Statistical Science.

If the codes were simply a matter random chance, then Gan's program would reveal this.

After testing the codes with this program, Gans

made the statement:

"The probability that these codes could appear by accident is virtually nonexistent."

One of the men most recognized for verifying the existence of the Torah codes in modern times is Eliyahu Rips, who is widely respected as one of the greatest mathematicians in the world and also known for his research in geometric group theory. However, it seems this code was discovered, to some extent, long before modern times.

The 13th-century Spanish Rabbi Bachya ben Asher described the process whereby the skipping of equal intervals of letters in the Torah could lead to obtaining divinely ordained information.

In the 18th century one of the greatest of the post biblical sages, Elijah Solomon, made the claim that all that was, is, and will be unto the end of time is included in the Torah.

The aforementioned are the opinions of some of the greatest Torah scholars of all time.

I find it interesting that encoded in Hebrew in the book of Genesis, in fifty-letter Skip sequences, we find the word Torah spelled out.

In Exodus this reoccurs with the same fifty-letter skip sequence. Then in Numbers and Deuteronomy we observed the same thing happening, only Torah is spelled backwards *(haroT)* in fifty-letter skip sequences.

As if Genesis and Exodus point in one direction with Numbers and Deuteronomy pointing in the opposite direction, all four books pointing to the center book in the Torah which is Leviticus.

It is as if the author wants us to focus on Leviticus. And when Leviticus was checked, they found the name *Yahweh* encoded in seven-letter skip sequences.

After running the numbers, they discovered that the probability of this happening by accident is less than one in three million.

As you continue reading, you will realize that this is just the beginning of the amazing discoveries to be found in the Torah.

We can find another clue to help solve this mystery in the meaning of the word "Hologram". The term is taken from the Greek words *holos* (whole) and *gramma* (message).

So, we have *"Whole Message."* God's Whole Message to man is His Word or the Bible.

Hebrews 11:3 KJV

Through faith, we understand that the worlds were framed by the word of God, so that things which are seen were not made of things which do appear.

People have always assumed that this verse just reaffirms that fact that God spoke creation into existence as demonstrated in the six days of creation.

But I believe this is one of those verses that has a dual meaning as we reflected on earlier:

"The world's were framed by the word of God."

We know the word of God is the Bible. So now this begs the question: could the Bible somehow be responsible for our very existence and the existence of the whole universe?

The very instructions given to the scribes as they copied God's Word by hand seems to confirm this idea.

"Even to this day, a Torah scroll is copied by hand from it's predecessor, written out according to unchanging rules, by scribes who undergo an exact detail course of training and preparation.

To each of them the following warning has been passed down through the ages; Should you perchance omit or add one single letter from the Torah, you would thereby destroy all the universe."

A passage written about the Torah by an 18th Century rabbi and "sage", Elijah Ben Solomon Zalman (17221797), called the Genius of Vilna says;

"The rule is that all that was, is, and will be, unto the end of time is included in the Torah, from the first word to the last word. And not merely in a general sense, but as to the details of every species and each one individually, and details of details of everything that happened to him from the day of his birth until his in."

The words of the genius of Vilna seem to echo the words of the much earlier Jewish "genius" - the greatest Rabbi of all time, Yahweh/Jesus- the Messiah. He said:

Matthew 5:18 NIV

"I tell you the truth, until heaven and earth disappear, not the smallest letter, not the least stroke of the pin, will by any means

disappear from the Law (the Torah) until everything is accomplished."

Source:
http://www.bibleprobe.com/biblecode.htm

This view of the Scriptures is different than our modern idea of the Bible. So long as the contextual meaning of the verses remain intact, we are not too concerned *with "the smallest letter."*

However, the statement of Jesus above shows an awareness that each individual letter is essential to the whole message (Hologram - author's note).

That is actually true of the Bible code. Since it involves exact mathematical precision, every letter must be in its place or the code will not work!

Surely, the above statement shows that the Son of God had supernatural awareness of the amazing depth of meaning in every letter of God's Word!

Could the next clue actually come from fallen angels?

The rich elite of this world get their guidance from Lucifer, who they admittedly worship, as well as other fallen angels.

Why do you think they know about all these end time events (obviously from a Satanic view point) which they put in so many of the recent movies?

What is the main purpose that angels are designed for? To be messengers. Fallen or not, they can't stop themselves from telling what they know any more than we can stop breathing.

Luke 1:19 ESV

And the angel answered him, "I am Gabriel. I stand in the presence of God, and I was sent to speak to you and to bring you this good news.

We have noted that *angelos* is the Greek word normally translated into English as "angel." Basically, *angelos* means "one who brings a message," and it often refers to human messengers as well as the heavenly host.

The biblical authors' use of *angelos* when recounting angelic appearances indicates that a chief task of these supernatural creatures is to bring a message from on high.

Source: *http://www.ligonier.org/learn/devotionals/angels messengers*

So, if I am correct, there should be a movie that reveals this Truth, still knowing that most will never get it. This movie is *The Matrix*.

The funny thing is if you go to the official Torah codes website *www.endtodarkness.com,* you will see the backdrop is almost identical to the green computer grid backdrop used in *The Matrix.*

We may be living in the Matrix, says *Engineer Epoch Times* -

October 31, 2014

Our world isn't necessarily a computer program designed by parasitic futuristic robots like in the movie *"The Matrix."* But it does bear a striking resemblance to a digital simulation or computer program, according to engineer Jim Elvidge.

Elvidge has worked with cutting-edge digital technology for decades. He holds a master's degree in electrical engineering from Cornell University as well as multiple patents in digital signal processing, and he has published papers about remote sensing and other related topics in peer-reviewed journals.

Combining his knowledge of digital systems with quantum mechanics, Elvidge has found that we may be living in something like a computer program.

> "The matter, the 'stuff' we seem to touch and feel, is actually, mostly, empty space. Our senses deceive us."

> "The entire universe is a cryptogram set by the Almighty." -Isaac Newton

What did Isaac Newton see in the Hebrew Bible that would cause him to make such a bold statement?

It's hard to say what a man with a genius mind who lived 300 years before the modern computer age would have discovered that would lead to such a proclamation.

However, by reviewing the statements made currently by men who have, and are, studying the Bible codes, using modern computer technology, we can find another clue to help us solve this mystery.

These men have discovered that the Torah code resembles a very advanced computer code, for lack of a better definition.

This is a program far more advanced than any quantum computer would run. Programs like *"The Bible Code"* (a modern computer program that helps one find codes in the Torah) can barely scratch the surface in a 2D format.

And I believe it was Micheal Drosnin that said they can see that the code goes 3D, but they are clueless as to how to access or crack it.

"'In the end', says Rips, 'the amount of information is incalculable and probably infinite. And that is only the first, crudest level of The Bible (mathematical) code.

"'We have always thought of The Bible as a book. We now know that was only its first incarnation. It is also a computer program.

"'Not merely a book that Eliyahu Rips typed into a computer, but something that its Original Author actually designed to be interactive and ever expanding.

"'The Bible code may be a timed series of revelations, each designed for the technology of its age'"

Daniel 12:4

But thou, O Daniel, shut up the words, and "seal" the Book (Revelation/Apocalypse 5:1-

5), [even] to the time of the end: many shall run to and fro, and [evil] knowledge (1 Timothy 6:20) *shall be increased.*

"It may be some form of information we cannot yet fully imagine, something that would be as strange to us now as a computer would have been to people 3,000 years ago.

'It is almost certainly many more levels deep, but we do not have a powerful enough mathematical model to reach it,' says Rips. 'It is probably less like a crossword puzzle and more like a HOLOGRAM.

""We are looking at two-dimensional arrays and we probably should look in at least three dimensions, but we don't know how.'"

No one can explain how the code was created. Every scientist, every mathematician and physicist who understands the code agree that not even the fastest supercomputers we have today - not even all of the computers now in the world working together - could have encoded The Bible in the way it was done 3,000 years ago.

"I can't even imagine how it would be done, how anyone could have done it," says Rips. "It is a mind beyond our imagination."

It is only logical to conclude that if one were to take the 3D Torah that forms our reality and copy it down in 2D as Moses did we would find all the details of our reality within this 2D copy.

I think there is enough evidence to propose that the Torah codes are the super high-tech program designed by God that makes up the holographic universe we live in - and indeed, our very existence.

I said before that Truth always brings loose ends together, makes more sense out of theories and fits the overall picture.

This would also explain why quantum physics shows our universe resembling a hologram. It would also explain why the Big Bang theory has been the best attempt, so far, to explain the origins of our universe. The projected hologram would resemble a Big Bang as the universe's beginning would be a projection of concentrated light which would then expand out from its point of origin.

CHAPTER 13
TAKING A CLOSER LOOK AT THE MILKY WAY GALAXY

If the Big Bang was an explosion of light when God said, *"Let there be light",* then we should be able to verify this somewhere in our universe.

So, this begs the question:

Is there anything we can observe in the universe that would be the equivalent of an enormous projection of light?

We have all heard of a black hole which seems to be the exact opposite of what we are looking for here. In theory, a black hole takes in all information and distributes it along the surface.

What we are looking for would be something that projects outwards (the Glory of God) which would resemble a vortex of light. So, in a sense, what we're looking for has all the attributes of the theoretical White hole.

The following is an excerpt from *http://nautil.us/ blog/white-holes-could-existbut-thatdoesnt- mean-they-do:*

Black holes are common in the cosmos- nearly every large galaxy harbors a supermassive one in its nucleus, not to mention smaller specimens. However, astronomers have yet to identify a single white hole.

That doesn't rule out their existence entirely since it might be hard to see one: if they effectively repel particles, there is a small possibility they could be lurking out there somewhere, invisible.

Nevertheless, none of all the diverse objects astronomers have observed seem to resemble what we'd expect from white holes.

The Big Bang actually works like a white hole in many respects, and maybe the closest our universe ever gets to having one. It lies in the past for any observer in the universe, and all we see expanded outward from it.

However, it didn't have an event horizon (meaning it was something called a "naked singularity", which is far less kinky than it sounds). Despite that, it resembles gravitational collapse in reverse.

So where do we even start when given the great expanse of the universe to look for this white hole?

I believe the Bible gives us clues as to where to start our search. The Bible indicates that Man and the Earth we live on are the apex or center of God's creation - and modern science confirms this.

The Modern World is Faced with the Breach of a Far-Reaching Paradigm.

Most cosmologists will not admit it publicly, but perhaps in private, they would tell you what is happening. Observations over the last 50 years, culminating with the Planck satellite results (March 2013) set modern science on a counter-revolution leading closer to ideas formed 500 years ago.

Today's cosmology is based on two broad principles: The Copernican Principle (we are not in a special place in the universe); and the Cosmological Principle (The Copernican

Principle, plus isotropy- the view from anywhere in the universe looks about the same).

Starting with early studies of the cosmic microwave background (CMB), and in recent years culminating with results from the COBE and then the WMAP satellites, scientists were faced with a signal at the largest scales of the universe - a signal that pointed right back at us indicating that we are in a special place in the universe.

Without getting overly technical, the Copernican and Cosmological principles require that any variation in the radiation from the CMB be more or less randomly distributed throughout the universe, especially on large scales.

Results from the WMAP satellite (the early 2000s) indicated that when looking at large scales of the universe, the noise could be partitioned into "hot" and "cold" sections and this partitioning is aligned with our ecliptic plane and equinoxes.

This partitioning and alignment resulted in an axis through the universe, which scientists dubbed "the axis of evil" because of the damage it does to their theories.

This axis is aligned to us. Lawrence Krauss commented in 2005:

"But when you look at [the cosmic microwave background] map, you also see that the structure that is observed, is in fact, in a weird way, correlated with the plane of the earth around the sun. Is this Copernicus coming back to haunt us?

"That's crazy. We're looking out at the whole universe. There's no way there should be a correlation of structure with our motion of the earth around the sun—the plane of the earth around the sun—the ecliptic. That would say we are truly the center of the universe."

Most scientists brushed the observation off as a fluke of some type, and many theories were created to explain it away. Many awaited the Planck mission.

The Planck satellite was looked upon as a referee for these unexpected (and unwelcome) results. The Planck satellite used different sensor technology and an improved scanning pattern to map the CMB.

In March 2013, Planck reported back, and in fact verified the presence of the signal in even higher definition than before!

There are cosmologists and scientists who

recognize the signal for what it is, and recent articles have started talking about the need for some "new physics" to explain the results.

Even on the Planck mission website, Professor Efstathiou states:

> "Our ultimate goal would be to construct a new model that predicts the anomalies and links them together. But these are early days; so far, we don't know whether this is possible and what type of new physics might be needed. And that's exciting"

Other observations have independently validated the "axis of evil" in recent years, and this adds credibility to the CMB observations. These observations include galaxy rotation alignments to our tiny part of the universe.

Very recent reports include observations of alignment between "sky distributions of powerful extended quasars and some other sub-classes of radio galaxies" and "a plane passing through the two equinoxes and the north celestial pole (NCP)".

Also, anisotropy of cosmic acceleration in Union2 Type 1(a) supernova appear to be aligning with the CMB features.

All this supports the contention that the Copernican Principle (and cosmological) have effectively been invalidated without even discussing the quantization of various astronomical features about us, which further support the contention.

The question is 'what will modern science do now'? Will they invent additional parameters to keep the current theories alive in addition to those already added: dark matter, dark energy, redshift as expansion, big bang inflation, etc.? Or will they consider the possibility that we are in a special place as observations clearly indicate?

Source: *www.medium.com/we-are-in-a-special-place*

If we are truly at the center of the universe, as the evidence clearly indicates, and the universe starts at the point of creation and then expands out from there, it would make sense that the source of the hologram should be somewhere in our own neighborhood. But do we have any evidence that this is the case?

The following is an excerpt from *http://physics.stackexchange.com:*

Could the black hole in the center of the galaxy be a white hole?

"In the center of the galaxy, there is a strong radio source which we call Sagittarius A*. Based on the high speed and orbit of nearby stars we have calculated that something with the mass of more than 4 million Sun's is located in this small area of space. And such a big mass in such a small area can only be a black hole, and the observed electromagnetic radiation comes from the accretion disk of the black hole.

"But there is also another solution to this method of logic deduction, Sagittarius A* might optionally be a white hole.

"Like black holes, white holes have properties like mass, charge, and angular momentum. They attract matter like any other mass, but objects falling towards a white hole would never actually reach the white hole's event horizon."

And if we look at the observations this solution seems to fit beautifully:

Sagittarius A* doesn't have any "appetite". The Chandra telescope observes a lot of gas close to Sag A*, and this gas is ejected outwards by an unknown mechanism.

We have never observed anything going into Sag A*, but based on the light given off by Sag A*, the researchers have calculated that less than 1% is "eaten" by the black hole and more than 99% is the ejected gas we observe.

The gas is not ejected outwards by gravitational slingshot effects as it is too close and has too little velocity. Tidal forces ejecting material is one hypothesis they are working on to explain this mystery.

If Sag A* is a black hole, it seems like there is some strange physics going on. If Sag A* is a white hole, ejection of material is what we would expect.

Light is flowing from a much larger area than a tiny accretion disk of a black hole.

If energy, matter, and antimatter is pouring in through Sag A*, this will create light.

The Chandra telescope did not observe the accretion disk which we expected to see with Chandra's high detail and resolution, but did observe only gas being ejected from Sag A*.

A large area around Sag A* is energized. A black hole doesn't energize nearby space much, but it mostly energizes a tiny accretion disk.

Close to the galactic center we observe the formation of many new stars. It is the most massive breeding ground for new stars in the galaxy and a large area close to the galactic center is populated by young stars.

A black hole would devour stars instead of giving birth to stars, while a white hole would give excellent conditions for star birth. Neither have we observed any star being devoured by Sag A*, or anything else, and we have observed it for 40 years.

In 2011 the scientists got excited. A huge cloud of gas called G2 was accelerating towards Sagittarius A*. They expected that the black hole would pull apart and devour the gas cloud and that the accretion disk of the black hole would light up.

But it was a big flop as the accretion disk showed no sign of lighting up and nothing extra was eaten, and it is a mystery that G2 was not ripped apart by the strong gravitational forces of the black hole.

Now they speculate if G2 actually is a star. and it is not feeding the black hole, could it instead feed itself?

We observe a large cloud of antimatter in the galactic center where the highest intensity of the signature frequency is at Sag A*.

If there is antimatter flowing in from the white hole, creation of antimatter by acceleration effects or the pure energy that creates antimatter and matter in a process similar to the Big Bang would explain the antimatter.

Today the antimatter is explained by being created by some binary X-ray stars close to the galactic center. But why do we then only see this behavior for these binary stars and not all the millions of others? They neither know how these stars potentially produce the antimatter nor why the amount is so high.

The universe is expanding at an accelerated speed. This requires energy to be added, and if energy pours in through white holes, energy is added.

We have never observed any singularity, so why should a black hole singularity exist?

Information seems to be lost in a black hole singularity - which goes against the rules of quantum mechanics. A white hole would be a solution to this black hole information paradox.

Two gigantic fermi bubbles extend up and down from the galactic center for at least 30,000 light years. These bubbles require vast amounts of energy to be created and can't be created by a slumbering black hole accretion disk.

So, the scientist suggests that the black hole had an eruption 2 million years ago. Instead of erupting black holes, a white hole could fuel the fermi bubbles.

If we just look at these observations, it might seem like they count in favor of Sag A* being a white hole. And it is an important question, as science is currently stuck with the option that Sag A* is a black hole singularity. If there is a white hole in the center of the galaxy instead, the implications are enormous, and it could give us answers to many grand problems in astrophysics.

Is it just coincidence that the only strong evidence we have in the entire universe for a white hole just happened to be in our neighborhood? I don't believe so.

We know there is deeper understanding the more time we spend searching out scripture (which always needs to be accompanied with prayer for the Lord's wisdom and guidance). Let's go to Job 36:22-33 and see if we can find biblical verification regarding the Milky Way.

Job 36:22-33 KJV

22 *Behold, God exalteth by his power: who teacheth like him?*

23 *Who hath enjoined him his way? or who can say, Thou hast wrought iniquity?*

24 *Remember that thou magnify his work, which men behold.*

25 *Every man may see it; man may behold it afar off.*

26 *Behold, God is great, and we know him not, neither can the number of his years be searched out.*

27 *For he maketh small the drops of water: they pour down rain according to the vapour thereof:*

28 *Which the clouds do drop and distil upon man abundantly.*

29 *Also can any understand the spreadings of the clouds, or the noise of his tabernacle?*

30 *Behold, he spreadeth his light upon it, and covereth the bottom of the sea.*

31 *For by them judgeth he the people; he giveth meat in abundance.*

32 *With clouds he covereth the light; and commandeth it not to shine by the cloud that cometh betwixt.*

33 *The noise thereof sheweth concerning it, the cattle also concerning the vapour.*

First of all, I want to point out that peeling back layers, or looking deep into scripture, ALWAYS has to be done with the guidance of the Holy Spirit to ensure that the information we are extracting is actually deeper revelation of God's truth and not taking things out of context, or worse, making it up as we go along.

That being said, let's dig into these eleven verses, one-by-one and see what we find.

Verse 22

Behold, God exalteth by his power: who teacheth like him?

Verse 22 starts by pointing out that nobody can come close to teaching like God.

Through God's power and word, we can get a much higher level of understanding. This verse is like a red flag signaling us to pay attention to the following verses where God will reveal some of His exalted teachings.

Verse 23

Who hath enjoined him his way? or who can say, Thou hast wrought iniquity?

This is making reference to the veil of darkness that God placed over our universe that is the law and brings entropy. Remember, Jesus sets us free from the curse of the law by taking on our *"iniquity."*

Isaiah 53:6 KJV

All we like sheep have gone astray; we have turned every one to his own way; and the LORD hath laid on him the iniquity of us all.

Verse 24

Remember that thou magnify his work, which men behold.

This is a clue that the following verses will magnify God's work. In most cases, when the Bible magnifies or wants us to see how awesome God's work is, it points us towards creation in general - and the heavens specifically.

There are examples of this throughout the Bible.

I will list a few.

Jeremiah 10:12 ESV

It is he who made the earth by his power, who established the world by his wisdom, and by his understanding stretched out the heavens.

Proverbs 3:19 ESV

The LORD by wisdom founded the earth; by understanding he established the heavens;

Isaiah 55:9 KJV

For as the heavens are higher than the earth, so are my ways higher than your ways, and my thoughts than your thoughts.

To further illustrate this point. I want to point out that Job 36:24 is literally saying, *"Remember that thou magnify his work"*. What is God's work?

Psalm 19:1 KJV

The heavens declare the glory of God; and the firmament sheweth his handywork.

The answer is the *heavens*, or *firmament* - another word for *heavens*.

Let's go to verse twenty-five.

> **25** *Every man may see it; man may behold it afar off.*

Once again, this is making reference to the heavens. However, it is getting more specific.

Depending on how good a man's eyes are and what time in history we are talking about, a different level of the heavens can be observed. Not all eyes are good enough to see most stars. However, even people with bad eyesight can usually see the Milky Way.

This is making reference to the cloudy formation that streams across the night sky that just about everyone with halfway decent sight can observe.

We will begin to recognize this as the Milky Way as we read on.

The verses that follow make this more clear. Let's continue to verse twenty-six.

> **26** *Behold, God is great, and we know him not, neither can the number of his years be searched out.*

This verse is just re-establishing the fact that no one understands the depth of how awesome

God is. Man cannot comprehend eternity. God is from *"everlasting to everlasting."* He is the *"Alpha and Omega."*

Verse 27

27 *For he maketh small the drops of water: they pour down rain according to the vapour thereof:*

We know the vapor that forms water as clouds. That is what this verse is talking about in the plaintexts.

The Milky Way appears as a cloudy formation that spans the night sky, and this is the deeper meaning.

Verse 28

28 *Which the clouds do drop and distil upon man abundantly.*

Obviously, in the plain text, this is making mention of the rain that comes from clouds. But at the deeper level, it is, once again, making reference to the Milky Way.

Verse 29

29 *Also can any understand the spreadings of the clouds, or the noise of his tabernacle?*

Now it's starting to get very specific at the deeper level. The cloudy formation that spreads across the night sky is the Milky Way.

If we remember what we went over earlier in the book, we will understand that the tabernacle of the Bride is described as being in the heavens. Let's take another look at that.

Psalm 19:4-6 KJV

4 Their line is gone out through all the earth, and their words to the end of the world. In them hath he set a tabernacle for the sun,

5 Which is as a bridegroom coming out of his chamber, and rejoiceth as a strong man to run a race.

6 His going forth is from the end of the heaven, and his circuit unto the ends of it: and there is nothing hid from the heat thereof.

Based on that information, we know that the spread-out cloudy formation can only be the Milky Way which is in the heavens where the tabernacle of the Bride is located.

Job 29 ends with: *"the noise of his tabernacle."*

Remember that when we searched the heavens and listened to the cosmic background noise, we discovered the voice of God in the location the Bible said it would be, making the exact sound the Bible said it would make.

I find it interesting that in Psalm 19 we discover that the heavens declare God's glory, and that His tabernacle is also located there. In Job, it seems to give us a more specific idea of where this sound and tabernacle come from - the Milky Way.

With that in mind, let's go to verse thirty.

30 *Behold, he spreadeth his light upon it, and covereth the bottom of the sea.*

God's glory is the light that is spread over the Milky Way and forms our reality.

His glory enters our reality from eternity by an interdimensional portal that is located at the center of the Milky Way. We went over this earlier and the next few verses in Job will confirm this. The scientific term for this would be a white-hole.

It is obviously important to remember the basics of how a hologram works if one is to reach a deeper understanding of our holographic reality by God's design.

The white-hole is the light that shines on and

projects the information, which is the veil of darkness or the Torah/Law - a literal sea of information.

Hypothetically, if you could reach the edge of the universe and then dive into this sea of information and swim to the very bottom at the other side, what would you find there?

You would find the awesome glory of God covering the bottom of the sea right before you went interdimensional and entered eternity.

Remember we are on verse 30. Let's look at it again.

30 *Behold, he spreadeth his light upon it, and covereth the bottom of the sea.*

Keep in mind that this sea is also the Law/Torah as we move on to verse 31.

31 *For by them judgeth he the people; he giveth meat in abundance.*

What does God use to judge the people which is also a curse or veil of darkness that was placed over our universe after the fall of Satan?

Galatians 3:10 KJV

"For as many as are of the works of the law

are under the curse: for it is written, Cursed is every one that continueth not in all things which are written in the book of the law to do them."

It seems ironic at first that the very one that represents the Law is the same one that sets us free from the curse of the Law, which is Jesus Christ - the Living Word of God.

Galatians 3:13 KJV

"Christ hath redeemed us from the curse of the law, being made a curse for us: for it is written, Cursed is every one that hangeth on a tree:"

The Law represents the perfection of God. Jesus is the mirror image of God and in fact, He and God are one and the same. Jesus is also the mirror image of the Law, which is the Torah, or Word of God. Jesus and the Law are one and the same, and both are perfect.

We can go right back to Psalm 19 to confirm this.

Psalm 19:7 KJV

The law of the LORD is perfect, converting the soul: the testimony of the LORD is sure, making wise the simple.

There is only one name under heaven that can convert your soul - and His name is Jesus Christ.

Acts 4:11 ESV

And there is salvation in no one else, for there is no other name under heaven given among men by which we must be saved.

Jesus represents the pyramid/tetrahedron at the quantum level that our holographic reality starts with, which is the head stone or capstone (the head of all four corners on a pyramid) on the New Jerusalem.

Acts 4:11-12 KJV

11 This is the stone which was set at nought of you builders, which is become the head of the corner.

12 Neither is there salvation in any other: for there is none other name under heaven given among men, whereby we must be saved.

We are the Builders that rejected Jesus Christ as the Head Stone in the first earth age. The physical evidence of this event can still be seen today when we look at the Great Pyramid and see that the capstone is missing.

This means we were the ones in need of redemption when the first age ended. Remember what we read in Isaiah 50:2?

Isaiah 50:2 KJV

Wherefore, when I came, was there no man? when I called, was there none to answer?

Is my hand shortened at all, that it cannot redeem? or have I no power to deliver? behold, at my rebuke I dry up the sea, I make the rivers a wilderness: their fish stinketh, because there is no water, and dieth for thirst.

Once we accept Jesus Christ as our personal Savior, God does not see our sin any more. From that point on, His Holy Spirit dwells inside us and God only sees the righteousness of Jesus Christ when He looks at us.

Isaiah 1:18 KJV

Come now, and let us reason together, saith the LORD: though your sins be as scarlet, they shall be as white as snow; though they be red like crimson, they shall be as wool.

Psalm 103:12 KJV

As far as the east is from the west, so far hath he removed our transgressions from us.

Now let's get back to Job 36:31.

31 *For by them judgeth he the people; he giveth meat in abundance.*

Jesus is the Law, but He is also *the Bread of Life.*

John 6:35 KJV

And Jesus said unto them, I am the bread of life: he that cometh to me shall never hunger; and he that believeth on me shall never thirst.

That's why Jesus commands us to feed His sheep with His word.

Now let's move on to verse 32.

32 *With clouds he covereth the light; and commandeth it not to shine by the cloud that cometh betwixt.*

In the plain text, this is easy to understand as we know the clouds come between us and the sun. But at the deeper level, it is explaining exactly what occurs at the center of the Milky Way Galaxy.

Scientist cannot get a good look at the Milky Way's center because of the thick cloudy-looking formation of stars that covers this area.

In other words, the clouds cover the light.

The following is an excerpt from http://www.aenigmatis.com/astronomy/find/sagittarius.htm:

> Sagittarius is home to a wealth of interesting astronomical objects.
>
> This is mainly due to the fact that, when we look at Sagittarius, we are looking towards the center of our own Milky Way Galaxy, where the density of stars and gas/dust clouds (nebulae) is greatest. Indeed, the actual center of the galaxy is located at the South-eastern corner of the constellation, hidden behind dark clouds of interstellar dust, close to the boundary with Scorpius. Under dark skies, the Milky Way glows distinctly in the region of Sagittarius.

You probably noticed that even in this excerpt, the dense star formation that blocks our view from the Milky Way's center is referred to as "dark clouds".

Scientist will go against the vast amount of obvious evidence (some of which we went over earlier in the book) that shows a white-hole at our galaxy's center, and they will call it a black hole because they have been told and taught that white-holes likely don't exist, and that black-holes are common, and most likely located in the center of spiral galaxies.

Even Astro Bob believes that there is a black-hole at the galactic center, because that's what Astro Bob has been conditioned to believe through the modern education system and mainstream media. Yet, Bob mentions that if you could remove the cloudy star formations, the center of the Milky Way would be so bright that it would cast shadows at night.

Here is what Bob has to say pertaining to this.

"Though the center remains hidden, large chunks of the Milky Way hover like clouds against the black sky. Every puffy piece is comprised of billions of distant stars the light of which blends together to form a misty haze. Here and there are smaller knots. These are individual gas clouds called nebulae and bright star clusters. A pair of 40-50mm binoculars will show many of these wonders and countless fainter stars plainly. If we could magically remove the dust between us and the galactic center, the rich intensity of stars in the Sagittarius direction would be bright enough to cast shadows at night."

Source: *astrobob.areavoices.com*

The following are a couple excerpts from *Wikipedia* on the center of the Milky Way or Sagittarius A.

> Sagittarius A or Sgr A is a complex radio source at the center of the Milky Way. It is located in the constellation Sagittarius, and is hidden from view at optical wavelengths by large clouds of cosmic dust in the spiral arms of the Milky Way.
>
> It consists of three components, the supernova remnant Sagittarius A East, the spiral structure Sagittarius A West, and a very bright compact radio source at the center of the spiral, Sagittarius A*.
>
> These three overlap: Sagittarius A East is the largest, West appears off-center within East, and A* is at the center of West.

Aenigmatis can't explain why..."the Milky Way glows distinctly in the region of Sagittarius."

Bob thinks it is due to... "the rich intensity of stars."

But it is actually way too bright to be caused by star clusters.

Wikipedia doesn't understand it either, so they admittedly use conjecture to explain it. Before I post the excerpt of their explanation Let's get the exact definition for "conjecture":

Merriam-Webster

Definition of CONJECTURE

1a: inference formed without proof or sufficient evidence;

  b: a conclusion deduced by surmise or guesswork.

Here's the excerpt trying to explain the white-hole from *Wikipedia*.

Sagittarius A East

This feature is approximately 25 light-years in width and has the attributes of a supernova remnant from an explosive event that occurred between 35,000 and 100,000 BCE. However, it would take 50 to 100 times more energy than a standard supernova explosion to create a structure of this size and energy.

It is conjectured that Sgr A East is the remnant of the explosion of a star that was gravitationally compressed as it made a close approach to the central black hole.

What they won't tell you is that they really don't have any evidence and they are just guessing (pun intended, as that's the definition of conjecture), because they have no idea why the center of our Milky Way is so bright and behaves like – well - like the white-hole that it is.

And lastly, verse thirty-three:

33 *The noise thereof sheweth concerning it, the cattle also concerning the vapour.*

In the plain text, this is telling how the cattle benefit from the rain.

At the deeper level, it is saying that the "noise" will show or give the evidence confirming the Law/Torah that is made from water and referenced in verse twenty-three of this chapter.

This is another clue that the water is moving. We can easily hear rushing water, but still water is silent. This noise is the voice of the Lord that we already listened to.

CHAPTER 14
THE NATURE OF REALITY

It's hard to establish biblical and scientific facts based on a holographic reality by God's design if one is still struggling to come to terms with the holographic nature of reality - especially when these facts help verify the three earth ages.

Hopefully, we can put that to rest in this chapter.

Understanding our reality will actually help us understand God's word better and to better understand creation by His design.

For example, this can help us wrap our minds around the fact that God is omnipresent.

"The day science begins to study nonphysical phenomena, it will make more progress in one decade than in all the previous centuries of its existence." -Nikola Tesla

When one realizes that reality is similar to a high-tech digital simulation or computer program, then one can come to terms with the fact that nothing that happens within this reality is by chance or accident.

What's more, one also realizes that God is aware of even the finest details, as they are all part of the program that He designed.

Not only did God design this program, but it works by His power - and literally through Him. This means God is actually part of the program, the central critical foundation of the program, or the pyramid-shaped quantum tetrahedron that represents Jesus Christ.

This explains why God has complete and total awareness of what occurs within our reality.

If a single grain of sand breaks free because of a slight breeze and tumbles a few feet on a beach, God is aware.

This is why the Bible says that even the number of hairs on your head are accounted for.

Luke 12:6-7 KJV

6 *Are not five sparrows sold for two farthings, and not one of them is forgotten before God?*

7 *But even the very hairs of your head are all numbered. Fear not therefore: ye are of more value than many sparrows.*

If reality is holographic, it would mean that everything in the universe is actually connected. Since we are within the code, vast distances and the physical are real to us.

However, at the quantum level, even vast distance would be meaningless as it is all connected and therefore instantly accessible.

At the quantum level, particles react instantly even when separated by vast distances.

If this concept seems a little far-fetched to you, I want you to consider what is known as quantum entanglement.

According to *Wikipedia,* quantum entanglement is a physical phenomenon that occurs when pairs or groups of particles are generated or interact in ways such that the quantum state of each particle cannot be described independently of the others, even when the particles are separated by a large distance—instead, a quantum state must be described for the system as a whole.

Measurements of physical properties such as position, momentum, spin, and polarization, performed on entangled particles are found to be appropriately correlated.

For example, if a pair of particles are generated in such a way that their total spin is known to be zero, and one particle is found to have clockwise spin on a certain axis, the spin of the other particle, measured on the same axis, will be found to be counterclockwise, as to be expected due to their entanglement.

However, this behavior gives rise to paradoxical effects: any measurement of a property of a particle can be seen as acting on that particle (e.g., by collapsing a number of superposed states) and will change the original quantum property by some unknown amount.

In the case of entangled particles, such a measurement will be on the entangled system as a whole.

It thus appears that one particle of an entangled pair "knows" what measurement has been performed on the other, and with what outcome, even though there is no known means for such information to be communicated between the particles, which at the time of measurement may be separated by arbitrarily large distances.

This is why all correct findings in real science will always point to Jesus and confirm God's word. Let me give a few examples of this.

In vortex math, there is a pattern that repeats itself. This pattern is 1,2, and 4 on one side, and 5, 7, and 8, on the other. This pattern is the grid that forms the energy that we pay for in the form of electricity. If you look at the grid you will notice that 3, 6, and 9 are outside of this pattern. This means 3, 6, and 9 do not have any resistance - or in other words, 3, 6, and 9 equal free energy.

Nikola Telsa knew this.

"If you knew the magnificence of the three, six and nine, you would have a key to the universe." –Nikola Tesla

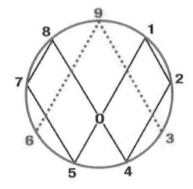

This is why the power and money-loving elitists suppressed Telsa's discovery of free energy.

Remember 3,6, and 9 represent free energy, or one could say, freedom. If you connect the 3, 6, and 9 you will get a pyramid. As we went over earlier, the pyramid represents Jesus Christ as the Headstone.

John 8:36 KJV

If the Son therefore shall make you free, ye shall be free indeed.

We can take this further and equate the free energy generated by 3, 6, and 9 that form the pyramid shape with Jesus Christ who offers us the only truly free gift that can save us.

"Salvation is only found in Jesus"

Acts 4:12 KJV

Neither is there salvation in any other: for there is none other name under heaven given among men, whereby we must be saved.

There are other things that we perceive in our reality that I do not believe are by chance.

The Bible says God is light.

1 John 1:5 KJV

This then is the message which we have heard of him, and declare unto you, that God is light, and in him is no darkness at all.

God/Jesus Christ are also described as *"Living Water"*.

Jeremiah 2:13 KJV

For my people have committed two evils; they have forsaken me the fountain of living waters, and hewed them out cisterns, broken cisterns, that can hold no water.

And also, **Jeremiah 17:13 KJV**

O Lord, the hope of Israel, all that forsake thee shall be ashamed, and they that depart from me shall be written in the earth, because they have forsaken the Lord, the fountain of living waters.

The appearance of the Glory of the Lord is said to be surrounded by a rainbow.

Ezekial 1:28 NASB

As the appearance of the rainbow in the clouds on a rainy day, so was the appearance of the surrounding radiance.

Such was the appearance of the likeness of the glory of the LORD. And when I saw it, I fell on my face and heard a voice speaking.

If we recall God's promise to Noah, it was to remember that when we see a rainbow, He will never flood the earth again. Now you know why He used a rainbow.

Genesis 9:11-13 KJV

11 *And I will establish my covenant with you, neither shall all flesh be cut off any more by*

the waters of a flood; neither shall there any more be a flood to destroy the earth.

12 *And God said, This is the token of the covenant which I make between me and you and every living creature that is with you, for perpetual generations:*

13 *I do set my bow in the cloud, and it shall be for a token of a covenant between me and the earth.*

Now, remember that God is *light* and Jesus Christ is *Living Water*.

When the light shines through the water we get a rainbow - God's promise to man to never destroy the world by flood again.

Do you think this is all just coincidence?

As you read on you will see that the coincidences just keep adding up.

The Bible says that God spoke our universe into existence. We know that the sounds of our voice are caused by the vibrations in our vocal cords. Sound is vibration and all physical matter is just energy vibrating at different frequencies.

"If you want to find the secrets of the universe, think in terms of energy, frequency and vibration." -Nikola Tesla

According to modern science, the universe formed faster than the speed of light and yet we know light travels faster than anything in existence. So how is that possible?

They will tell you that this is due to cosmic inflation.

However, this is just their way of inventing an explanation for something of which they have absolutely no idea. Without the word of God as a guideline, and since God is the Creator, all they can do is speculate.

Yes, they do invent totally fabricated ideas with absolutely no basis in reality to explain things which they don't understand.

Dark matter is one example of this, and the multi-universe is another very good example.

So why did they invent the multi-universe hypothesis? Simply put, it is because our universe is a holographic reality that leaves no room for error. What do I mean by that?

Leonard Susskind, theoretical physics at Stanford University, in a YouTube interview titled *"Leonard Susskind - Is the Universe Fine-Tuned for Life and Mind?"* had this to say;

> "'Everything seems to be almost on a knife's edge. If you were to change the laws of physics even a little bit the world as we know it wouldn't exist."

> The host goes on to ask Leonard: "How many of these constants or laws of physics would fit into this category of fine tuning?" The host then says, "Let's talk about one in particular, the cosmological constant".

> Leonard's response was; "That's the one that is really on a knife's edge.

> "It is on such a narrow knife edge that it is almost inconceivable, if you were to change it just the tiniest, tiniest bit we could not be here."

How tiny you ask yourself? Leonard says it is one part in a zillion, zillion, zillion, etc., eventually equaling one-hundred and twenty-three zeros to one. It's beyond any mathematical possibility of chance.

Why is it beyond any possibility of chance? Because when you exist in a holographic program, nothing happens by chance.

For example, it is not by chance that the original Greek definition of Hologram is *"Whole Message"* and God's Word is His whole message to mankind and God's Word, The Torah/Law, is literally what forms our holographic reality.

Modern science can only hypothesize about reality being similar to a holographic projection. But, as Christians that believe the word of God is one-hundred percent truth, we don't need to hypothesize about the make-up of our reality because the Bible tells us exactly how reality is formed, down to the finest details, and real science will always confirm God's Word.

For example, you can take a holographic plate (the film or plastic card that a holographic image is stored on) - let's say it's a hologram of a bird that is on the plate - and you can cut it into pieces.

After you have cut it into pieces you will find that each piece still contains the complete image, the bird in this example, that forms the hologram.

Photo   Hologram

Now let's apply this holographic fact to our own reality based on real science and God's word.

Our reality is made in the image of God/Jesus Christ who represents the pyramid shape. If you were to cut our reality into the finest pieces that make it up, the Planck Length formed pyramid, each piece would still contain the complete image of our reality which is Jesus Christ - or the quantum level pyramid shape.

This could explain how God is omnipresent in our universe.

This does not mean that Jesus isn't also God in the flesh who came to our fallen holographic reality as a man and paid the price for our sins.

Holographic does not mean less real. Our reality is very real to us and we are accountable for everything we do in our reality. Jesus knew this, and He also knew that He was our only chance at redemption.

Genesis 1:27 KJV

So God created man in his own image, in the image of God created he him; male and female created he them.

We find the image of Jesus Christ in the smallest division that forms our reality which brings us back to Colossians 1:16-18.

Colossians 1:16-18 KJV

16 *For by him were all things created, that are in heaven, and that are in earth, visible and invisible, whether they be thrones, or dominions, or principalities, or powers: all things were created by him, and for him:*

17 *And he is before all things, and by him all things consist.*

18 *And he is the head of the body, the church: who is the beginning, the firstborn from the dead; that in all things he might have the preeminence.*

It is not by chance that every detail of verses 16-18 line up with the position, shape, and function of the pyramid shape and light at the quantum level.

John 1:4 KJV

In him was life; and the life was the light of men.

So how is it possible that every detail of the universe we exist in can be found in the Bible that is at least 2,000 years old even in the New Testament text?

It is because the spoken Word of God truly is the source code that forms our reality. This is the reason that they can find codes in the 2D version of the Torah that contains the details of what goes on in our reality.

This is also the reason the Bible suggest two different versions of the same Torah: The one that was taken down by Moses directly from the mouth of God; and the one that God actually used to speak our reality into existence.

The Messiah, Jesus Christ, is literally the Word, the Perfect Law, and light that forms our reality!

John1:1-4 KJV

1 In the beginning was the Word (Jesus Christ), and the Word was with God, and the Word was God.

2 The same was in the beginning with God.

3 All things were made by him; and without him was not any thing made that was made.

4 In him was life; and the life was the LIGHT of men.

CHAPTER 15
THE MARS/EARTH CONNECTION

As we went over earlier in the book, the Bible mentions three earth ages. This is a very difficult area of research because of the fact that the end of an earth age means that an extinction-level event occurred. The first earth age ended from a large asteroid impact. Most people know this as the impact that they are told took place 65 million years ago and killed off the dinosaurs.

This impact happened as a direct repercussion from God destroying Satan's home planet after Satan became prideful. The Bible calls this planet Rahab.

Job 26:11-13 KJV 1900

"The pillars of heaven are stunned at His rebuke. He quiets The sea with his power, and by his understanding, He shatters (maw-khats, dashes asunder), Rahab, by His spirit the heavens were beautiful; His hand forbids the fugitive snake."

From Earth, Rahab would be bright enough to be seen in the daytime and would have dominated the night sky, hence where the name Lucifer as light bearer may have gotten its origin.

The planet was solid because diamonds bearing carbonaceous asteroids appear as the debris of its destruction.

The planet was very likely a water-bearing planet, since a high percentage of water is seen in comets. This has been verified in the book *Dark Matter, Missing Planets & New Comets*. Van Flandern states that the parent body of the asteroids once sustained oceans and an atmosphere.

The Elite are aware of the first earth age because their knowledge originates with the one they worship, Satan/Osiris. Some prophets of the Bible also know of the different earth ages from the Spirit of God that revealed it to them. Two of these individuals, from the Old Testament, are Job and Isaiah.

A few things from the different earth ages tend to repeat themselves. For example, God has wiped clean the memories of man in our current age so that he cannot recall things (from memory) during the first earth age. Job mentions this.

Job 8:8-9 KJV

8 *"For inquire, I pray thee, of the former age, And prepare thyself to the search of their fathers.*

9 *(For we are but of yesterday, and know nothing. Because our days upon earth are a shadow:)"*

And the memories of those that enter the next earth age will also be wiped clean. Isaiah mentions this.

Isaiah 65:17 KJV

"For, behold, I create new heavens and a new earth: and the former shall not be remembered, nor come into mind."

We are given some critical clues concerning the first earth age and our current age in **Job 8:9a**.

"For we are but of yesterday..."

"Yesterday" is making reference to the first earth age. This seems to suggest that we somehow came from the first earth age.

Many believe Job is the oldest book in the

Bible. If this is the case, and Job is referencing a former age, there is no other logical biblical conclusion that we can reach.

> "**The Pentateuch** (the first five books of Moses) would have been written after the time of the Patriarchs, so Job would be, by default, the oldest book in the Bible. ... You'll be hard pressed to find another **Old Testament** book that does that and doesn't mention Jews or Hebrews at all."

> Source: *https://www.quora.com/How-do-people-know-that-Job-is-the-oldest-book-of-the-Bible*

Job 8:9b *"...and know nothing. Because our days upon earth are a shadow"*

I believe this is referring to our current earth age.

Remember that the first age was - and the last age will be - designed to be eternal and lit by God's Glory. It is only our current earth age that is *"Framed by the Word of God"* - which is the veil/Torah.

Our current age is holographic and has entropy where everything withers, decays and eventually dies.

Our holographic reality makes our days on earth like a "shadow" when compared to the eternal reality of the first and last ages.

And *"know nothing"* means that we don't remember anything from the previous earth age.

We currently see a very small part of reality when compared to eternity, just as Paul mentions in 1 Corinthians 13:12:

1 Corinthians 13:12 ESV

"For now we see in a mirror dimly, but then face to face. Now I know in part; then I shall know fully, even as I have been fully known."

We know that God placed Lucifer/Satan in charge of Rahab/Astera, Mars, and the earth during the first earth age.

Obviously, Astera was destroyed and its remains make up the asteroid belt. This leaves us with Mars and the Earth to examine and compare to see if there is any evidence that these two planets are linked in the distant past by having similar ancient civilizations and the same Leader.

Ezekiel 28 is one of the several scriptures in the Bible that have a duel reference, as we went over, comparing Satan to the King of Tyre.

At first glance, the prophecy in Ezekiel 19 seems to refer to a human king. The city of Tyre was the recipient of some of the strongest prophetic condemnations in the Bible. Tyre was known for building its wealth by exploiting its neighbors.

Ancient writers referred to Tyre as a city filled with unscrupulous merchants. Tyre was a center of religious idolatry and sexual immorality.

The biblical prophets rebuked Tyre for its pride which was brought on by its great wealth and strategic location. It seems to be a particularly strong indictment against the king of Tyre in the prophet Ezekiel's day, rebuking the king for his insatiable pride and greed.

However, some of the descriptions in Ezekiel go beyond any mere human king. In no sense could an earthly king claim to be *"in Eden"* or to be *"the anointed cherub who covers"* or to be *"on the holy mountain of God."*

Therefore, most Bible interpreters believe that is a dual prophecy, comparing the pride of the king of Tyre to the pride of Satan.

Some propose that the king of Tyre was actually possessed by Satan, making the link between the two even more powerful and applicable. Before his fall, Satan was indeed a beautiful creature.

He was perhaps the most beautiful and powerful of all the angels.

The phrase *"guardian cherub"* possibly indicates that Satan was the angel who "guarded" God's presence as the "Covering Cherub" of that time period, that would have been depicted on the first ark (of the Covenant).

Pride Led to Satan's Fall.

Rather than give God the glory for creating him so beautifully, Satan took pride in himself, thinking that he himself was responsible for his exalted status. Satan's rebellion resulted in God casting Satan from His presence and will, eventually, result in God condemning Satan to the lake of fire for all eternity.

Source: *http://www.gotquestions.org/King-of-Tyre.html*

What I find very interesting is that the ancient city of Tyre in which Satan was Prince is also the earthly capital of Cydonia/Sidonia.

Cydonia is the city on Mars that NASA's Viking 1 snapped photos of. Satan was also the Prince of Cydonia on Mars.

There are websites that claim the Face on Mars, Cydonia are simply natural formations, but my research has shown this to be highly improbable - if not totally impossible.

For you doubters, I suggest you read *PROOF THAT THE CYDONIA FACE ON MARS IS ARTIFICIAL*, which can be found at

http://www.metaresearch.org/solar %20system/cydonia/proof_files/proof.asp.

And for further proof of a Mars/Earth connection, I highly recommend that you watch David Flynn's video, *AOD 2003 -David Flynn - Mars/Earth Connection: Cydonia, Genesis 3, Part 1* on YouTube.

Like I mentioned before, you could easily write a book on this topic alone. The website reference and the David Flynn video explain in depth the pictures and historical evidence I will list.

I will start with the beginning of our current earth age in the Garden of Eden.

A lot of people wrongly assume that the fruit of the tree of the knowledge of good and evil was an apple. But if you study history, you will find out that the evidence suggests the fruit was actually a quince. David Flynn explains this in detail on his YouTube video *The Mars-Earth Connection*.

Quince from *Wikipedia*, the free encyclopedia:

The quince (/ˈkwɪns/; Cydonia *oblonga*) is the sole member of the genus Cydonia in the family Rosaceae (which also contains apples and pears, among other fruits). It is a small deciduous tree that bears a pome fruit, similar in appearance to a pear, and bright golden-yellow when mature.

Notice the name of the fruit is Cydonia - *oblonga*. The name of the city on Mars is Cydonia.

It is also very interesting that the name of the city in Egypt, *"Ciaro"*, means *Mars*.

Cairo \ca(i)-ro\ as a boy's name is pronounced *KIE-ro*. It is of Arabic origin, and the meaning of Cairo is *"victorious"*; Place name: the name of the capital of Egypt, derived from *"al Qahir"*, the Arabic name of the planet Mars.

When you slice open the quince you find a pentagon shape and five-pointed star in its center.

When you look at the pyramid on Mars in Cydonia you find the same exact shape.

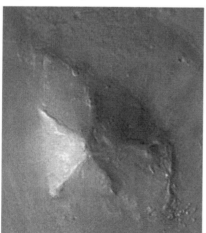

So, we can see that the fruit center and the Pyramid have the same shape. The fruit and the city of the pyramid have the same name as well. But it goes a lot further than this.

Most people think of the number 666 as representing Satan in human form, and the pentagon shape is used by cults to represent Satan during dark rituals.

It is also interesting that during the transit form west to east of the annular eclipse, the frequency of 666 Hertz generates a cymatic pattern in the shape of a pentagon as demonstrated on YouTube.

You can view this short video clip by going to YouTube and typing in "The Oh-No! Man Cymatic pattern 666 hertz."

The U.S. Pentagon also takes on this shape and represents the U.S. Military, or Power to wage war.

The Pentagon is the headquarters of the United States Department of Defense located in Arlington County, Virginia. As a symbol of the U.S. military, "the Pentagon" is often used metonymically to refer to the U.S. Department of Defense.

Mars was the god of war in Roman mythology.

MARS - GENDER: Masculine - USAGE: Roman Mythology - PRONOUNCED:

MAHRZ (English) [key] Meaning & History

Possibly related to Latin mas "male" (genitive maris). In Roman mythology, Mars was the god of war, often equated with the Greek god Ares. This is also the name of the fourth planet in the solar system.

Source:
www.behindthename.com/name/mars

The Pentagon, as well as several other five-star symbols, are frequently used by the Illuminati and Freemasons who consider themselves enlightened.

They certainly know of the first earth age as it was ruled by their god Lucifer, and the significance of these symbols that were in use since before recorded history.

I also find it amazing and beyond chance that Mars Cydonia is almost an exact match for Earth's Avebury, England, down to the exact same angles and landmarks.

One of the primary angles is 19.47 which is also the date of the Roswell incident.

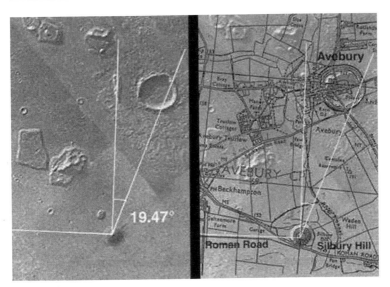

Mars, Cydonia | Avebury, England

I suspect there was also a third Cydonia on Lucifer's home planet of Rahab. Lucifer was placed in charge of Rahab, Mars, and earth, by God.

God destroyed Rahab and therefore it is impossible to make that comparison. However, we can obviously see the evidence of an ancient Cydonia on Mars and Earth.

So, you can see that the evidence clearly shows several links between Earth and Mars from the ancient past.

This makes perfect sense when we remember that Lucifer was in charge of all the nations and kingdoms of the first earth age.

Isaiah 14:12-13 KJV

12 *How art thou fallen from heaven, O Lucifer, son of the morning! how art thou cut down to the ground, which didst weaken the nations!*

13 *For thou hast said in thine heart, I will ascend into heaven, I will exalt my throne above the stars of God: I will sit also upon the mount of the congregation, in the sides of the north*

Keep in mind that the first age was designed to be eternal and the age to come will be eternal. So, who is going into this final/eternal earth age and what kind of bodies will they have?

1 Corinthians 15:54 NLT

Then, when our dying bodies have been transformed into bodies that will never die, this Scripture will be fulfilled: "Death is swallowed up in victory."

"Our dying bodies" - That means all of us who put our faith and trust in Jesus Christ who currently live in bodies of flesh that die.

So what kind of bodies will we be given? *"... transformed into bodies that will never die".*

We will be given eternal bodies. It makes sense that an eternal age would require an eternal body.

So, who came from the previous earth age and what kind of bodies did they have?

The first age was designed to be eternal. I don't think it takes much of a leap to conclude that the bodies of those that existed at that time would have been designed to be eternal and the same, or very similar, as the bodies that we will be given during the next earth age. So, who existed during the first earth age?

Let's reflect on what we went over.

Job 8:8-9 KJV

8 *"For inquire, I pray thee, of the former age, And prepare thyself to the search of their fathers.*

9 *(For we are but of yesterday, and know nothing. Because our days upon earth are a shadow:)"*

What age is Job asking us to inquire about?

"For inquire, I pray thee, of the former age."

The first earth age.

And who came from this age?

"...we are but of yesterday". We did!

Something that never ceases to amaze me is the fact that so many Christians believe we will enter into the next earth age and be given eternal bodies and yet, they will totally reject the idea that we came from the previous age and had bodies that were designed to be eternal.

Because they do not understand the "Bigger Picture", they will claim this idea goes against scripture and the verse they almost always reference is **Hebrews 9:27 (KJV)** *"And as it is appointed unto men once to die, but after this the judgement"*

They will claim that we could not have been here during a previous age and then born into this age because man only dies once.

The Bigger Picture:

Man only dies in our current earth age. Eternal bodies do not die. Man did not die in the first age and he will not die in the next age. So, this claim does not contradict scripture, as man only dies once in our current age.

You may have noticed that in every instance where the Bible mentions the end of the first earth age it says, *"there was no man."*

It never says that man died. It is as if God removed them because of their rebellion, but He did not charge them yet because the Law was not in place at this time.

(I will give more biblical evidence confirming that God removed and rescued mankind from the oppression of Lucifer in the final chapter of this book.)

Then, at birth, we enter this fallen age that is under the Law and we are found guilty, and all who don't receive the free gift offered by the Redeemer, Jesus Christ, are condemned.

This is not teaching reincarnation, because we were not born into the first age. We are only born into our current age. Just as we will not be born into the age to come. We will be given mature adult (eternal) bodies.

This is not teaching Calvinism, because all of us are here to make a choice to either accept or reject Jesus Christ as Lord and Savior.

If this is true and we rebelled along with Satan during the first earth age, then why are we given a second chance that Satan was not given?

To understand this, we need to remember that

things tend to repeat themselves in some of the earth ages. The Eden account with Adam and Eve is a reflection of what happened during the first earth age.

Adam and Eve rebelled and disobeyed God, but they were given a second chance because they were influenced or deceived by Satan.

Who was in charge of the first age? Satan/Lucifer. So, we would have been under Satan's rule and influenced or manipulated by him. Satan was not given a second chance because he was not influenced, manipulated, or deceived by anyone.

This is 100% scriptural. However, people usually dismiss all the Bible verses that make reference to this because it goes against their conditioning or what they have been taught.

What did Jesus say?

John 10:34 NIV

"Jesus answered them, Is it not written in your law, I said, Ye are gods?"

No, this is not teaching Mormonism.

Context! Jesus is making reference to **Psalm 82:6 (KJV)**

"I have said, Ye are gods; and all of you are children of the most High."

This Psalm is in the Old Testament. The children of the Most High that were *"gods"* in the Old Testament were often angels (beings designed by God to be eternal) or "the sons of God'.

Job 1:6 KJV

"Now there was a day when the sons of God came to present themselves before the LORD, and Satan came also among them."

Angels are referred to as gods with a lower case *"g"*. Even the ancient Greeks had their own version of this story, albeit, from a pagan stance. They too referred to the fallen angels (the 200 angels that had sexual relations with the women on earth) as *"gods"*, and the Nephilim giants that were a result of the sin of these fallen angels were referred to as *demi-gods* by the Greeks.

This is because angels were beings that were designed by God to be eternal.

I believe *"gods"* is simply making reference to beings that are immortal or created to be eternal.

I do not think we were angels, as some believe, I think we were men and women that had bodies similar to the bodies Christians will be given in the age to come.

To verify this, we simply need to consider the fact that Jesus was talking to men in John 10:34.

John 10:34 KJV

Jesus answered them, Is it not written in your law, I said, Ye are gods?

And when the Bible mentions this account, it always mentions, *"there was no man."* It never says that there weren't any angels.

The body is the physical vessel that contains our spirits. God created our immortal bodies in the first age and then breathed life into them in the same way that He created Adam's flesh body in our current age and then breathed life into him. Therefore, the natural or physical body would always have to be created first and 1 Corinthians 15:46 only confirms this.

The body is just a physical vessel for our spirits. In an eternal age, the natural body would be an eternal body just as the natural body for our current age is a flesh body.

Here is the definition of *"Natural"*.

nat·u·ral - ˈnaCH(ə)rəl / SubmitSubmit - adjective

1.existing in or caused by nature; not made or caused by humankind.

"carrots contain a natural antiseptic that fights bacteria"

2. of or in agreement with the character or makeup of, or circumstances surrounding, someone or something.

This is conclusive evidence that it was man that had eternal bodies in the first age.

Jeremiah 4:25 KJV

I beheld, and, lo, there was no man, and all the birds of the heavens were fled.

Isaiah 50:2 KJV

Wherefore, when I came, was there no man? when I called, was there none to answer? Is my hand shortened at all, that it cannot redeem? or have I no power to deliver? behold, at my rebuke I dry up the sea, I make the rivers a wilderness: their fish stinketh, because there is no water, and dieth for thirst.

A very important fact to take note of is that God does not have a redemption plan for angels and in Isaiah 50:2, right after He says there was no man, He says, *"is my hand shortened that I cannot redeem?"*

This is the entire reason behind God's redemption plan!

The next verse that some will claim is scripture which contradicts what I am saying is Romans 5:12.

Romans 5:12 KJV

Wherefore, as by one man sin entered into the world, and death by sin; and so death passed upon all men, for that all have sinned:"

They will say that this verse proves that sin originated with Adam and therefore we are all guilty because we are related to him.

Let's examine this.

Psalm 145:17 KJV

"The LORD is righteous in all his ways, and holy in all his works."

Isaiah 61:8 NKJV

"For I, the Lord, love justice ..."

Not one person reading this book can honestly tell me that if my grandpa murdered someone, it would be righteous and just to put **me** to death because of what **he** did.

So why would it be righteous and just for God to put all of us to death for what Adam did? If you are honest then you know the answer is that this would not be just at all.

I understand that there are generational curses and that physical death is passed down from Adam through reproduction. This is because a dead spirit is not compatible with an eternal body.

This is why Adam was thrown out of Eden when his spirit died, or when "death entered". He was placed under the law where his physical body would eventually die.

The death of our spirits is a direct result of our own actions when we rejected Jesus as the Head-Cornerstone or Capstone in the first earth age. We are then born into this fallen age with fallen flesh bodies.

We have living souls but dead spirits until we are born again. Only Christ can bring life to our spirits.

1 Corinthians 15:45 NASB

So also it is written, "The first MAN, Adam, BECAME A LIVING SOUL." The last Adam became a life-giving spirit.

So, does this mean scripture contradicts itself, or that God is above His own rules and laws? Absolutely not!

Adam was set up for failure from the beginning. Yes, it was a divine setup.

I can prove this through scripture. Adam was made from the dust of the earth, or in other words, he was given a perfect body made of flesh and blood. Some people believe that if Adam had never sinned by eating the forbidden fruit, we would all be living in a perfect world today. This was never God's plan. Flesh and blood cannot inherit the kingdom of God.

1 Corinthians 15:50 KJV

Now this I say, brethren, that flesh and blood cannot inherit the kingdom of God; neither doth corruption inherit incorruption.

Jesus came to earth (God in the flesh) and followed the Law to the letter, and was the only person to have ever done so.

So, let's re-examine Romans 5:12 in context and see what it I actually saying.

12 *"Wherefore, as by one man sin entered into the world ..."*

The key word here is *"entered"*. Something cannot *"enter"* unless it already exists.

Sin did not originate with Adam. Sin originated with Satan/Lucifer during the first earth age. Adam did not even exist at the time.

We sided with Lucifer before the foundations of our current age existed.

This is why Jesus was considered crucified *from the beginning* for all of us who choose Him during this age.

We were the *"Builders"* that rejected Jesus as the *"Head Cornerstone"* in the first earth age.

Keep in mind that the latest studies in quantum physics indicate that the smallest form that makes up the building blocks of reality (the Planck Length) is in the shape of a tetrahedron or pyramid.

Earlier in this book, we went over the fact that a lot of people mistakenly think that the New Jerusalem is the shape of a giant cube.

They get the cube shape from this verse, Revelation 21:16: *"And the city lieth foursquare, and the length is as large as the breadth: and he measured the city with the reed, twelve thousand furlongs. The length and the breadth and the height of it are equal."*

However, the key to understanding the true shape of the New Jerusalem is in the details of this verse. *"The city LIETH foursquare".*

A cube is squared regardless of if you are looking at it from the top, bottom, or sides, but a pyramid is only squared at the base or the part that "Lieth" on the ground. A pyramid is also the same length, width and height in keeping with the measurements given for the New Jerusalem.

We, as Christians, represent the body of the pyramid and Jesus Christ represents the Head or Capstone.

The Capstone is still a complete pyramid without the body, but the body can never be complete without the Head or Capstone (Jesus Christ).

All four corners of a pyramid meet at the top, or the Head, Capstone. This literally makes the Capstone the *"Head of the Corner".*

Acts 4:11 BLB

"This is 'the stone having been rejected by

you, the builders, which has become the head of the corner."

This would make the shape that represents Jesus Christ a tetrahedron when referencing our current age, or the smallest building block that forms our current creation/reality.

Colossians 1:16-18 KJV

16 *"For by him were all things created, that are in heaven, and that are in earth, visible and invisible, whether they be thrones, or dominions, or principalities, or powers: all things were created by him, and for him:*

17 *And he is before all things, and by him all things consist.*

18 *And he is the head of the body, the church: who is the beginning, the firstborn from the dead; that in all things he might have the preeminence."*

Revelation 13:8 KJV

And all that dwell upon the earth shall worship him, whose names are not written in the book of life of the Lamb slain from the foundation of the world.

This is because we were here with Jesus before our current earth age ever began.

Ephesians 1:4 KJV

According as he hath chosen us in him before the foundation of the world, that we should be holy and without blame before him in love

2 Timothy 1:9 DBT

...who has saved us, and has called us with a holy calling, not according to our works, but according to his own purpose and grace, which was given to us in Christ Jesus before the ages of time.

It says, *"before the ages of time"*. There isn't any time in an eternal age. Time did not exist in the previous age and it will not exist in the age to come.

Time is exclusive to our current, fallen age. In fact, time is a critical part that pertains to entropy in this fallen age in which we exist.

1 Peter 1:20 ESV

He was foreknown before the foundation of the world but was made manifest in the last times for the sake of you.

Adam was created in a body of flesh, in a neutral state. This means that Adam had freedom of choice.

He could choose to do right or wrong. Adam was placed in a perfect environment, the Garden of Eden.

Adam was a vessel of flesh in which sin entered into this earth age. As soon as this occurred, God kicked Adam out of the Garden.

The Garden of Eden is in a different, perfect dimension. This is why it has not been, and never will be discovered during this earth age.

God restored the earth during our current age to perfection and pronounced it good.

However, this age was restored under the veil of darkness that was put in place after Satan's fall. This veil brings entropy and decay. This is why Adam was thrown out of the garden - a perfect environment in another dimension here on earth - into a world that was mourning and decaying.

Jeremiah 4:28 KJV

For this shall the earth mourn, and the heavens above be black: because I have spoken it, I have purposed it, and will not repent, neither will I turn back from it.

The very next phrase in the verse is *"and death by sin"* - because the wages of sin (that entered through Adam and originated in the previous age) is death.

The verse goes on to say:

"... and so death passed upon all men ..."

This means that death is passed on through the fallen flesh by means of reproduction. We are all descendants of Adam by flesh relation. When Adam sinned, his flesh, or DNA, became corrupted and from that point on all flesh was cursed with eventual death. However, the spiritual portal into this earth age is birth, or through the vagina.

As we went over, Lucifer/Satan knows this, and this is part of the passed down "enlightenment", which means the Elite are aware of this, and this is part of the "Truth hidden in plain sight". This is why the Elite Catholic leaders prioritize the portal, "Mary", over the Redeemer, "Jesus Christ". Several Catholic pictures of Mary are actually vaginas or portals.

I am sorry if this seems to get a little redundant, but it seems people sometimes have a very difficult time letting go of false beliefs that they have heard preached for several years.

Some will argue that we could not have existed

in a previous age because the Bible says that the flesh came first and then the spirit afterward.

1 Corinthians 15:46 KJV

Howbeit that was not first which is spiritual, but that which is natural; and afterward that which is spiritual.

The body is the physical vessel that contains our spirits. God created our immortal bodies in the first age and then breathed life into them in the same way that He created Adam's flesh body in our current age and then breathed life into him. Therefore, the natural or physical body would always have to be created first and 1 Corinthians 15:46 only confirms this.

It is possible that our eternal bodies are seated with Christ in heavenly places (see Ephesians 2:6) and we will put these eternal bodies back on upon entering the next age. We can put on our clothes in the morning because our clothes already exist.

1 Corinthians 15:54 KJV

So when this corruptible shall have put on incorruption, and this mortal shall have put on immortality, then shall be brought to pass the saying that is written, Death is swallowed up in victory.

Jesus was our first love in the previous age. He died to restore that relationship.

We fell in the first age and we are given a second chance in our current age where we start with fallen bodies of flesh and a sinful spirit from conception and our first works are sinful.

So, I don't see how Jesus could be considered our first love in our current age. I believe Jesus was making reference to the first age when He addresses the church.

Revelation 2:4-5 (KJV)

4 Nevertheless I have somewhat against thee, because thou hast left thy first love.

5 Remember therefore from whence thou art fallen, and repent, and do the first works; or else I will come unto thee quickly, and will remove thy candlestick out of his place, except thou repent.

This is why Jesus Christ is the Redeemer.

"Redeem is wider in its application than ransom, and means to buy back, regain possession of, or exchange for money, goods, etc."

Source: Redeem / Define Redeem at *Dictionary.com*
www.dictionary.com/browse/redeem

You cannot "buy back" something unless you already owned it at some point.

Adam was created neutral with the ability to choose. Once we accept Jesus Christ as our Savior, we are "born again". This is because Jesus paid a heavy price for our salvation/redemption.

1 Corinthians 6:20 KJV

"For ye are bought with a price: therefore glorify God in your body, and in your spirit, which are God's."

We had a relationship with Jesus during the first earth age where we previously existed, like Adam did in our current age, in a neutral state with the ability to choose right or wrong (do not get this confused with a "sin nature").

Like Adam, we let Satan influence, or manipulate, us into making a very bad decision to rebel against God.

We enter into this world through the flesh portal, the vagina, already having a sin nature due to our rebellion in the first age, and here are given another chance to choose or reject Jesus Christ.

Once we choose Jesus Christ as our Savior, we are redeemed or bought back, and our relationship with Jesus Christ is restored.

However, since Jesus had to pay a price by coming in the flesh and dying on the cross and then conquering death when He arose three days later, we are no longer "neutral".

At this point (once we are born again), Jesus has paid a price for us and we are His property. If you purchase something, it becomes your possession or property. At the point we are born again, our bodies become the Temple of God.

He is the head of the Temple (the capstone) and we are the base (the body) just like the New Jerusalem shows.

Jesus is the capstone that we rejected in the first earth age, just like the Great Pyramid shows. Who did we reject and side with instead? Lucifer/Satan. Who is depicted as now replacing the capstone that we rejected on the US dollar bill? Horus/Satan in the flesh. When we are born again, we are bought back - or purchased - and this is why we are sealed unto the day of redemption.

Ephesians 4:30 (KJV)

"And grieve not the holy Spirit of God, whereby ye are sealed unto the day of redemption."

We will still have a sin nature as long as we are in fallen (flesh) bodies, but our spirits are secured, purchased, and the property of Jesus Christ.

Jesus restored the relationship out of His great love and mercy.

But why would He do this for us? Why was this relationship so important to Him? Because this was a Husband/Wife relationship. Once the relationship is restored, we are the Bride of Christ!

Revelation 21:2 KJV

2 *"And I John saw the holy city, new Jerusalem, coming down from God out of heaven, prepared as a bride adorned for her husband."*

Ephesians 5:25 KJV

"Husbands, love your wives, even as Christ

also loved the church, and gave himself for it"

CHAPTER 16
CONNECTING THE INFORMATION

Now let's put everything together: The Bible (in context); true history: and real science - and see how it all plays out.

Genesis 1:1-2 KJV

1 In the beginning God created the heaven and the earth.

2 And the earth was without form, and void; and darkness was upon the face of the deep. And the Spirit of God moved upon the face of the waters.

Genesis 1:1 is simply a statement declaring that God created everything (the heavens and the earth) at the very beginning.

In Genesis 1:2 the earth became without form and void and was placed in a state of darkness and flooded with water as a judgement from God.

We are going to take a very close look at this using first the Word of God, and then we will examine this using real science and observable history.

Obviously, darkness is associated with God's judgement and curses. We also know that the Bible says..."*This then is the message which we have heard of him, and declare unto you, that God is light, and in him is no darkness at all."* **1 John 1:5**

So, it does not seem to make sense that a God of Light would start out His creation with a formless void that is covered in water and enshrouded by darkness.

I find it interesting that there is another passage in the Bible that starts out saying (almost verbatim) what Genesis 1:2 says, and then it goes on to say that God will not make a *"full end"* and finishes by saying that this is the reason for the darkness we currently have as a backdrop to creation.

Jeremiah 4:23-28 KJV

23 *"I beheld the earth, and, lo, it was without form, and void; and the heavens, and they had no light.*

24 *I beheld the mountains, and, lo, they trembled, and all the hills moved lightly.*

25 *I beheld, and, lo, there was no man, and all the birds of the heavens were fled.*

26 *I beheld, and, lo, the fruitful place was a wilderness, and all the cities thereof were broken down at the presence of the Lord, and by his fierce anger.*

27 *For thus hath the Lord said, The whole land shall be desolate; yet will I not make a full end.*

28 *For this shall the earth mourn, and the heavens above be black; because I have spoken it, I have purposed it, and will not repent, neither will I turn back from it."*

Whatever happened here caused the heavens to have no light and seems to have brought an end (removal, not death) to the type of humans that previously existed. *"... the heavens, and they had no light." "I beheld, and, lo, there was no man."*

It would be silly to mention that there was no light and man due to God's fierce anger unless both light and man previously existed.

So, if there was a previous earth age, then this would mean the heavens and earth are actually very old. A lot of Christians are ignorant of this fact. We will see if the Bible supports this and then we will see if we can find out what caused God to become so angry as to end the first age.

2 Peter 3:5-7 KJV

5 *"For this they willingly are ignorant of, that by the word of God the heavens were of old, and the earth standing out of the water and in the water:*

6 *Whereby the world that then was, being overflowed with water, perished:*

7 *But the heavens and the earth, which are now, by the same word are kept in store, reserved unto fire against the day of judgment and perdition of ungodly men."*

A lot of Christians seem to think this is making reference to the Flood of Noah.

We know that the Bible is very clear in telling us that a few people and thousands of animals survived the flood of Noah.

Most of the same Christians that believe this also believe that the heavens and earth are about 6,000 years old. Which on the grand scale of things is actually very young. The above reference clearly says two things:

#1 *"For this they willingly are ignorant of, that by the word of God the heavens were of old";*

#2 *"Whereby the world that then was, being overflowed with water, perished".*

It clearly says the world is old and that it perished. This does not give any indication that anything or anyone was left after this event.

Notice it says that the "world" that existed then perished. It does not say that the humans that existed at that time died. It is making reference to the heavens and earth that existed. This is made clear when looked at in context with the next verse.

So how do we know that this was a destruction of a previous earth age? **CONTEXT!**

In the very next verse it says that by the same word, our current heavens and earth will be destroyed by fire. Why would it mention our current heavens and earth, by the same word, are going to be destroyed by fire unless it was making reference to our first heaven and earth being destroyed?

This has profound implications once we realize that the Word, in the form of Water, is what destroyed the first age, and our current, holographic, reality is now formed by the same Word.

Therefore, once the Word is rolled up like a scroll, our current age will be exposed to the fullness of God's glory and will be destroyed by fire.

Let's move on to **verse 7**:

"But the heavens and the earth, which are now, by the same word are kept in store, reserved unto fire against the day of judgment and perdition of ungodly men."

We must take into account that Jeremiah clearly says that whatever caused God's fierce anger is also what brought on God's judgment and the reason that the heavens are black. We need to also remember that 2 Peter says the previous earth was destroyed by water. This would have been a raging flood that would have made the flood of Noah pale by comparison.

This begs the question: What caused God's fierce anger?

The answer to this question can be found in **JOB 26:11-13**:

"The pillars of heaven are stunned at His rebuke. He quiets The sea with his power,

and by his understanding He shatters (maw-khats, dashes asunder), Rahab, by His spirit (or Glory-author's note)) the heavens were BEAUTIFUL; His hand forbids the fugitive snake."

So, what/who caused God's fierce anger and whom did He rebuke/forbid?

Satan! - or "the fugitive snake."

Why was God so angry with Satan?

Because Satan took on pride and tried to make himself equal to God. This is likely where the saying, *"Pride cometh before a fall"*, originated.

Isaiah 14:13-14 KJV

13 *"For thou hast said in thine heart, I will ascend into heaven, I will exalt my throne above the stars of God: I will sit also upon the mount of the congregation, in the sides of the north:*

14 *I will ascend above the heights of the clouds; I will be like the most High."*

So would God destroy the first earth age because of Satan's pride? It was because Satan was placed in charge of the first earth, along with Mars and Rahab, by God.

As far as I have ever known, if anyone has a throne they also have a kingdom.

"I will exalt my throne above the stars of God".

Remember the first earth was destroyed by a flood worse than that of Noah's day. This is the reason why God calming the sea is mentioned along with Satan's rebuke in this same passage.

"He quiets the sea with his power."

We must also remember that when this account is mentioned in Jeremiah it says, *"the heavens, and they had no light."*

And in the account of this event in Job, it says;

"by His Spirit the heavens were BEAUTIFUL"

In the previous age, the heavens were lit by God's Glory and they were beautiful. But after God's judgment of Satan, He removed His Glory or light.

This was at the same time God stretched the veil of darkness over our current reality/earth age/universe as mentioned in the same passage in Jeremiah.

"For this shall the earth mourn, and the heavens above be black."

Satan's home planet was Astra/Rahab. We can see that in this same passage in Job. It says *"He (God) shatters (mawkhats, dashes asunder), Rahab."*

As we covered earlier, there is actual detailed evidence of this event that we can still observe today in our solar system.

What we see today as the Asteroid belt is what remains of the planet Astra.

Now we have come full circle. The first earth age was destroyed by water when God rebuked Satan.

"Whereby the world that then was, being overflowed with water, perished."

God calmed the water: *"He quiets the sea with his power."*

But God said that He will *not make a full end* in the last verse we read of this account in **Jeremiah 4:27:**

"For thus hath the Lord said, The whole land shall be desolate; yet will I not make a full end."

This brings us to the creation account of our current age mentioned in Genesis 1:2:

"And the earth was without form, and void; and darkness was upon the face of the deep. And the Spirit of God moved upon the face of the waters."

This is right before God created Adam and Eve and told them to *"replenish"* the earth. Why would God tell them to *replenish* the earth unless something had already previously existed?

Genesis 1:28 KJV

"And God blessed them, and God said unto them, Be fruitful, and multiply, and replenish the earth, and subdue it: and have dominion over the fish of the sea, and over the fowl of the air, and over every living thing that moveth upon the earth."

The word *"replenish"* here is the same word (in Hebrew) used in the same context as when God told Noah to *replenish the earth.*

Genesis 9:1KJV

"And God blessed Noah and his sons, and said unto them, Be fruitful, and multiply, and replenish the earth."

This only makes sense if there was a previous earth age.

The Bible confirms that God did not start the earth *without form and void*. He originally made the earth to be inhabited.

Isaiah 45:18 KJV

> *For thus saith the LORD that created (bara, created a new thing) the heavens; God himself that formed (yatsar, moulded into a form, as a potter does) the earth and made (asah, fashioned, prepared) it; he hath established (kun, formed) it, he created (bara) it not in vain (tohu, ruin), he formed (yatsar, moulded into a form) it to be inhabited.*

Genesis starts out, *"IN the beginning God created (bara) the heaven (literally, heavens) and the earth."* This was a long, long time ago.

The Earth itself is very old. Then sometime later, but before Adam was created, *"earth was (hajah, had become) without form (tohu, ruin), and void (bohu, empty); and darkness was upon the face of the deep."* This catastrophe was the result of a divine judgment upon Satan.

We already read where it mentions the rebuke

of Satan at the end of the first age in Job. But Job seems to mention the first age in several places.

It seems that certain things in the different earth ages tend to repeat themselves.

We are in our current earth age (the 2nd earth age) and we have no memory of the previous earth age. This seems to be mentioned in Job 8:8-9.

Job 8:8-9 KJV

8 *"For enquire, I pray thee, of the former age, and prepare thyself to the search of their fathers:*

9 *(For we are but of yesterday, and know nothing, because our days upon earth are a shadow:)"*

And likewise, when we enter the next earth age, we will not remember our current earth age - Isaiah 65:17.

Isaiah 65:17 KJV

"For, behold, I create new heavens and a new earth; and the former things shall not be remembered, nor come into mind."

We already went over how the first earth age

(before God put the veil of darkness over our current universe) was beautiful and lit by God's Glory.

The last earth age will once again be beautiful and lit by God's Glory.

Isaiah 60:19 KJV

"The sun shall be no more thy light by day; neither for brightness shall the moon give light unto thee: but the LORD shall be unto thee an everlasting light, and thy God thy glory."

Revelation 21:23 KJV

"And the city had no need of the sun, neither of the moon, to shine in it: for the glory of God did lighten it, and the Lamb is the light thereof."

The first age was lit by God's Glory and was designed to be eternal or without entropy, and the last age will once again be lit by God's Glory and will be eternal and without entropy. It is only our current age (under the veil) that decays and has entropy.

We came from the previous age of glory and all who receive Jesus Christ as their Redeemer and Savior will return to glory in the age to come when Jesus removes the veil of darkness.

2 Corinthians 3:18 NASB

"But we all, with unveiled face, beholding as in a mirror the glory of the Lord, are being transformed into the same image from glory to glory, just as from the Lord, the Spirit."

The reason why our current age is under the veil (the scientific reason, as we know God placed the veil over our universe as a result of Satan's pride) was explained in God's Word and through quantum physics.

This explains why our universe is 99% darkness. God put our universe under a veil of darkness after the fall of Satan.

Eternity beyond this veil radiates with light or the Glory of God. This means that the true default position is light.

This Veil of Darkness is the source-code designed by God that forms our current reality.

God Spoke our current universe/age into existence.

It makes sense that the Hebrew Torah "The Spoken Word of God" would be the source code beneath all reality.

This is what the Bible clearly says in the plain text.

Hebrews 11:3 KJV

"Through faith we understand that the worlds were framed by the word of God, so that things which are seen were not made of things which do appear."

We can see it says the worlds were framed by the Word of God. But what does it mean by *"things which are seen were not made of things which do appear."*

It was demonstrated in this book how quantum physics shows that what we think of as solid matter is actually just positive and negative forces in atoms. Therefore, everything in our reality that we see is made from things that we cannot see.

Let's continue to review what we went over so that we get a better perspective pertaining to how this played out based on God's word and scientific findings.

The Bible actually contains the details on how our reality is generated in the plain text. The Bible says that *"the worlds were FRAMED by the Word of God."*

Leonard Susskind of the Stanford Institute for Theoretical Physics (who is not a Christian, and as far as I know does not even believe in God) tells how our reality resembles a hologram in his YouTube video titled *"Leonard Susskind on The World as Hologram"*.

He goes on to say that the advanced math and science indicates that this hologram is generated by a film-like layer that contains the information - or source code. He goes on to say that this film surrounds - or "FRAMES" - our universe and is in the cosmic background.

If our reality is formed by the Torah, which is a written and very high tech code, then it makes sense, like computer code, that if you remove any part of the code, the program will collapse. In the case of this code, it would mean that our reality would cease to be, or it would pass away. This is exactly what Jesus said.

Matthew 5:18 KJV

"For verily I say unto you, Till heaven and earth pass, one jot or one tittle shall in no wise pass from the law, till all be fulfilled."

But what does Jesus mean when He says, *"Till heaven and earth pass"?*

The Torah was written on a scroll, and it is a black veil or curtain/tent that surrounds our universe. Jesus will roll up this scroll at the end of this age and our current reality will dissolve - or cease to exist.

This will be when our current heaven and earth will *"pass away"*.

Isaiah 34:4 KJV

"And all the host of heaven shall be dissolved, and the heavens shall be rolled together as a scroll: and all their host shall fall down, as the leaf falleth off from the vine, and as a falling fig from the fig tree."

The Torah - or veil/curtain - that God used to form our reality is actually a curse that God put in place after the fall of Satan. This curse separates our reality from the Light - or Glory of God - which is eternity beyond the veil/Torah.

Before the fall of Satan, the heavens were lit by Gods Glory and they were beautiful.

JOB 26:11-13

"The pillars of heaven are stunned at His rebuke. He quiets The sea with his power,

and by his understanding He shatters (maw-khats, dashes asunder), Rahab, by His spirit the heavens were BEAUTIFUL; His hand forbids the fugitive snake."

Eternity beyond the veil of darkness that frames our universe is lit by God's glory.

Psalm 113:4 KJV

The LORD is high above all nations, and his glory above the heavens.

Now our reality is formed by - and under - the Torah/veil of darkness. But when Jesus rolls the heavens/Torah up like a scroll, our reality will once again be lit by God's Glory.

Isaiah 60:19 KJV

"The sun shall be no more thy light by day; neither for brightness shall the moon give light unto thee: but the LORD shall be unto thee an everlasting light, and thy God thy glory."

Revelation 21:23 KJV

"And the city had no need of the sun, neither of the moon, to shine in it: for the glory of God did lighten it, and the Lamb is the light thereof."

So, we had bodies that were designed to be eternal, and we came from the former age that was lit by God's glory. Those of us that receive Jesus Christ as our Lord and Savior will return to glory in the age to come.

2 Corinthians 3:18 KJV

"We all, with unveiled faces, are looking as in a mirror at the glory of the Lord and are being transformed into the same image from glory to glory; this is from the Lord who is the Spirit."

The Bible mentions this veil in several places. I will give a few examples.

Isaiah 50:3 KJV

"I clothe the heavens with blackness, and I make sackcloth their covering."

Why *sackcloth?*

Smith's Bible Dictionary:

Sackcloth - cloth used in making sacks or bags, a coarse fabric, of a dark color, made of goat's hair.

Sackcloth and ashes were used in Old Testament times as a symbol of debasement, mourning.

When someone died, the act of putting on sackcloth showed heartfelt sorrow for the loss of that person.

We see an example of this when David mourned the death of Abner, the commander of Saul's army (2 Samuel 3:31).

Jacob also demonstrated his grief by wearing sackcloth when he thought his son, Joseph, has been killed (Genesis 37:34).

These instances of mourning for the dead mention sackcloth, but not ashes.

So, sackcloth is a fitting description for the veil of darkness God stretched over the universe as He mourned the fall of Satan and the repercussions that followed.

The Bible also calls the veil of darkness a tent that God stretched over the heavens.

Isaiah 40:22 KJV

> *"It is he that sitteth upon the circle of the earth, and the inhabitants thereof are as grasshoppers; that stretcheth out the heavens as a curtain, and spreadeth them out as a tent to dwell in:"*

After the fall of Satan, God destroyed the former reality and made the earth *"without form and void"*. And he removed His Glory or light at the same time he put the veil of darkness in place. This is why the heavens - or universe - is black when we look up at the night sky.

Jeremiah 4:23 KJV

"I beheld the earth, and, lo, it was without form, and void; and the heavens, and they had no light."

Jeremiah 4:28 KJV

"For this shall the earth mourn, and the heavens above be black: because I have spoken it, I have purposed it, and will not repent, neither will I turn back from it."

So why would the Law - or Torah - be black and used as a curse? Because the Law - or Torah - is a curse to all who are not in Christ.

Galatians 3:10 KJV

"For as many as are of the works of the law are under the curse: for it is written, Cursed is every one that continueth not in all things which are written in the book of the law to do them."

Galatians 3:13 KJV

"Christ hath redeemed us from the curse of

the law, being made a curse for us: for it is written, Cursed is every one that hangeth on a tree:"

The Sages have been told from the beginning, when copying the Torah, that if they make one mistake, they are to burn it because it is the equivalent of destroying the universe.

The universe is a cryptogram set by God Almighty. -Isaac Newton

Reality is merely an illusion, albeit a very persistent one. -A. Einstein.

"If quantum mechanics hasn't profoundly shocked you, you haven't understood it yet. Everything we call real is made of things that cannot be regarded as real." – Niels Bohr.

CHAPTER 17
CHRIST AND THE CHURCH

(THE GREAT MYSTERY)

Christ and the church is an amazing biblical mystery that, once solved, not only proves we came from the first earth age, but it will actually give the biblical verification of the exact source from which we were created during the first earth age.

To help us understand the conclusion we need to keep a few key points in mind.

#1 Our reality is just a dim mirror reflection of the eternal order just as scripture says.

1 Corinthians 13:12 NLT

Now we see things imperfectly, like puzzling reflections in a mirror, but then we will see everything with perfect clarity. All that I know now is partial and incomplete, but then I will know everything completely, just as God now knows me completely.

Let's take a look at the same verse in the World English Bible translation.

1 Corinthians 13:12 WEB

For now we see in a mirror, dimly, but then face to face. Now I know in part, but then I will know fully, even as I was also fully known.

There is also another verse that mentions our reality as if looking in a mirror, but it goes on to give us clues regarding the first and final earth ages that were and will be lit by God's glory.

2 Corinthians 3:18 NASB

But we all, with unveiled face, beholding as in a mirror the glory of the Lord, are being transformed into the same image from glory to glory, just as from the Lord, the Spirit.

#2 The Eden account is also a reflection of the eternal order.

This is especially important in order to fully understand the Garden of Eden account and how it applies to many other things in the former age as well as the age to come.

#3 Christians are the bride of Christ.

This is very important. When it is applied to Ephesians 5:22-32, we not only get a deeper understanding of how a husband and wife relationship should work, but we can even understand how this applies to Christ and the Church.

#4 Christ is the Head of the body, which is the Church.

Not only does this let us know Christ's position pertaining to the church, but it also lets us know the shape He represents at the quantum level.

This shape is the pyramid shape or Chief Cornerstone, Capstone.

This is the first building block in all reality, both eternal and our currently fallen reality. This would mean that Jesus Christ literally comes before all things.

This brings us to our fifth and final point to keep in mind.

#5 Jesus is literally the Foundation of all reality.

As we already went over, this is demonstrated in several Bible verses and it is critical to grasp in order to get a better understanding of the eternal order and the Bible as a whole.

I will give a few scripture references that confirm this before we dive into this great mystery.

Colossians 1:16-18 KJV

16 *For by him were all things created, that are in heaven, and that are in earth, visible and invisible, whether they be thrones, or dominions, or principalities, or powers: all things were created by him, and for him:*

17 *And he is before all things, and by him all things consist.*

18 *And he is the head of the body, the church: who is the beginning, the firstborn from the dead; that in all things he might have the preeminence.*

John 1:1-4 KJV

1 *In the beginning was the Word, and the Word was with God, and the Word was God.*

2 *The same was in the beginning with God.*

3 *All things were made by him; and without him was not any thing made that was made.*

4 *In him was life; and the life was the light of men.*

Keeping all five aforementioned points in mind, let's dive into this great biblical mystery!

In the Garden of Eden, God created Adam - a reflection of Jesus Christ. This especially applies to the eternal order.

The Bible calls Jesus Christ *the Last Adam*.

1 Corinthians 15:45 NLT

The Scriptures tell us, "The first man, Adam, became a living person." But the last Adam-- that is, Christ--is a life-giving Spirit.

We know that Eve was the bride of Adam. When we apply this to the eternal order, we can understand that the Church, or all true Christians, are the bride of Christ.

It is important to take a closer look at Ephesians 5:22-32 in order to see what God's word says and apply it towards solving this mystery.

Ephesians 5:22-33 KJV

22 *Wives, submit yourselves unto your own husbands, as unto the Lord.*

23 *For the husband is the head of the wife, even as Christ is the head of the church: and he is the saviour of the body.*

24 *Therefore as the church is subject unto Christ, so let the wives be to their own husbands in every thing.*

25 *Husbands, love your wives, even as Christ also loved the church, and gave* *himself for it;*

26 *That he might sanctify and cleanse it with the washing of water by the word,*

27 *That he might present it to himself a glorious church, not having spot, or wrinkle, or any such thing; but that it should be holy and without blemish.*

28 *So ought men to love their wives as their own bodies. He that loveth his wife loveth himself.*

29 *For no man ever yet hated his own flesh; but nourisheth and cherisheth it, even as the Lord the church:*

30 *For we are members of his body, of his flesh, and of his bones.*

31 *For this cause shall a man leave his father and mother, and shall be joined unto his wife, and they two shall be one flesh.*

32 *This is a great mystery: but I speak concerning Christ and the church.*

Now let's break it all down, verse by verse, and see what we can discover.

Verse 22

"Wives, submit yourselves unto your own

husbands, as unto the Lord."

Wives are to submit to their husbands as unto Jesus Christ because He is the Head of the bride - or church. This is verified in the very next verse.

Verse 23

"For the husband is the head of the wife, even as Christ is the head of the church: and he is the saviour of the body."

When we apply Christ's position as the Head of the Church, and we remember that the Church also represents the body - or Pillar - of the New Jerusalem, we can know that Christ represents the Pyramid shaped Capstone - or Head.

Verse 24

"Therefore as the church is subject unto Christ, so let the wives be to their own husbands in every thing."

This lets the wife know her position in the marriage relationship. But most importantly, it lets us, as Christians, know our position pertaining to Christ. We are to submit to the will of Jesus in all things.

Verse 25

"Husbands, love your wives, even as Christ also loved the church, and gave himself for it;"

Not only does this give us an idea of the extent to which a husband should love his wife, but it reminds us of what Jesus was willing to do in order to redeem His bride.

Verse 26

"That he might sanctify and cleanse it with the washing of water by the word,"

This verse has deeper implications than most realize when we apply it to what we have learned regarding the first earth age and the veil of darkness, which is the Word in the form of water.

This water was used to destroy and cleanse the first age and to also form our current age after God divided the waters from the waters.

The waters above the firmament contain the information that is projected to form our current reality.

This is also represented through baptism where we have life that then dies and is cleansed by water, and then experiences resurrection through Jesus Christ.

Not only are we resurrected by Jesus when we are born again, but our fallen age will also be resurrected by Jesus when He removes - or rolls up - the veil of darkness at the end of this fallen age.

The three earth ages represent Life, Death, and Resurrection.

All creation is formed by and revolves around Jesus Christ.

However, verse 26 actually has even deeper implications. Let's take another look at it.

> **26** *"That he might sanctify and cleanse it with the washing of water by the word,"*

This verse is talking about Christ cleansing the Church by the *washing of water by the word*.

We know Jesus is the word. We also know that Jesus shed His water and blood to cleanse us when the Roman soldier pierced His side.

John 19:34 KJV

> *But one of the soldiers with a spear pierced his side, and forthwith came there out blood and water.*

As you read on, you will discover that the cleansing blood and water necessarily came from the same area that the offenders (the church) were created from.

Verse 27

"That he might present it to himself a glorious church, not having spot, or wrinkle, or any such thing; but that it should be holy and without blemish."

Jesus paid the price for our sins. After we make Jesus our Lord and Savior, God sees us as righteous because He looks at us through the blood of Jesus that cleanses us as white as snow.

It is important to realize that this offense, by us, was committed during the first age. When the Bible talks about us sinning and falling, it uses the past tense. It doesn't say all will eventually sin and fall. It says all have already sinned and are fallen beneath the veil of darkness that separates us from the eternity that is lit by God's glory.

This is why Jesus is called *"Redeemer"* - meaning to buy-back. It is not by chance that this is exactly what Romans 3:23-24 says.

Romans 3:23-24 ESV

23 for all have sinned and fall short of the glory of God,

24 and are justified by his grace as a gift, through the redemption that is in Christ Jesus

Let's move on to verse twenty-eight.

Verse 28

"So ought men to love their wives as their own bodies. He that loveth his wife loveth himself."

Men are to love their wives as their own bodies because the two become united as one through Marriage. This also applies to Jesus Christ and His bride who are united during the marriage of the Lamb.

Even though we will be united with Christ as one body, we are still subject to Christ in all things because He is still the Head of the body, just as the husband is head of the wife.

Verse 29

"For no man ever yet hated his own flesh; but nourisheth and cherisheth it, even as the Lord the church"

This is further verification that we are part of the flesh, or body, of Christ.

Verse 30

"For we are members of his body, of his flesh, and of his bones."

This verse is a critical clue in solving the *"great mystery"* which lets us know where we came from.

Remember, the Eden account is a reflection of the eternal order. Once we realize this and apply it to the Eden account, we find biblical verification of our origin.

There are two verses in Genesis regarding the Eden account that say exactly what verse 30 just said, and what verse 31 will say.

We find this in Genesis 2:23-24. Let's take a look!

Genesis 2:23-24 KJV

23 *And Adam said, This is now bone of my bones, and flesh of my flesh: she shall be called Woman, because she was taken out of Man.*

24 *Therefore shall a man leave his father and his mother, and shall cleave unto his* *wife: and they shall be one flesh.*

As far as I know, this is the first time this biblical mystery has been solved. I realize this will take some people out of their comfort zones because of that fact alone, they have never heard this before. However, it is exactly what the Bible says.

Let's compare Ephesians 5:30-31 with Genesis 2:23-24.

Ephesians 5:30-31 KJV

30 *For we are members of his body, of his flesh, and of his bones.*

31 *For this cause shall a man leave his father and mother, and shall be joined unto his wife, and they two shall be one flesh.*

Genesis 2:23-24 KJV

23 *And Adam said, This is now bone of my bones, and flesh of my flesh: she shall be called Woman, because she was taken out of Man.*

24 *Therefore shall a man leave his father and his mother, and shall cleave unto his wife: and they shall be one flesh.*

We literally came from a part of Christ's body (His rib) and we, as Christians, will be united with Him.

God formed Eve from a part of Adam's body (his rib) in the same way that He created us, during the first earth age, from a part of Christ's body.

Let's go back to Ephesians 5:29 to confirm this.

Verse 29

"For no man ever yet hated his own flesh; but nourisheth and cherisheth it, even as the Lord the church:"

Now let's move on to the final verse we are going to look at in Ephesians.

Verse 32

"This is a great mystery: but I speak concerning Christ and the church."

Verse 32 literally tells us that this is the *"great Mystery"* and that it is about Christ and the church.

This mystery has been solved and it truly is awesome!

Some of you will reject this simply because you haven't heard it before. Some will reject it because they have placed an All-Knowing, All-Mighty, Eternal God in a box based on man's limited perspective.

There is something very interesting that I would like to point out.

Remember that I said I feel that the sons of God mentioned in the Bible are beings that were designed to be eternal. This would include angels as well as mankind, or all of us, with our original eternal bodies.

Earth was created for mankind from the very beginning. And when Lucifer rebelled there was a great war. Could this be why the sons of God shouted for joy after Satan and a third of the angels that joined him were defeated right before God laid the foundations for our current earth age?

Yes, we rebelled too in the sense that we listened to Lucifer and did not finish the capstone of the Great Pyramid. We rejected the very piece that represented Jesus.

However, Lucifer hated us because we were created from the side of Christ and he wasn't. After we rejected the capstone we fell under great oppression by Satan and his angels. It was Christ that removed and rescued us from this oppression and then let us witness the restoration of the earth where we would be given a second chance.

There is biblical verification for this. Let's take another look at Isaiah 19:19-20.

Isaiah 19:19-20 KJV

19 In that day shall there be an altar to the Lord in the midst of the land of Egypt, and a pillar at the border thereof to the Lord.

20 And it shall be for a sign and for a witness unto the Lord of hosts in the land of Egypt: for they shall cry unto the Lord because of the oppressors, and he shall send them a saviour, and a great one, and he shall deliver them.

I Realize that a lot of people think of Isaiah 19:19-20 as making reference to Moses delivering the Israelites from the Egyptians and others think of it as a prophecy regarding Egypt. I don't deny that both the aforementioned situations are possible.

As we went over earlier in the book, God oftentimes includes past events, especially regarding Lucifer and the first earth age, with future prophecies in the same chapters.

First, I will ask the obvious question.

Why, and how, could the Great Pyramid possibly be "*a sign and for a witness unto the Lord*" in relation to Moses and the Israelite's exodus from Egypt?

I can't find any biblical, or otherwise, relevant connections that would link Moses and the Israelite's exodus from Egypt in relation to the Great Pyramid being "*a sign and for a witness unto the Lord*". As a matter of fact it is just the opposite.

If you believe what the Bible clearly says regarding the Great Pyramid, that it was built as "*an altar to the Lord*", it would eliminate any possibility of the Egyptians or any other pagan nation being responsible for it's construction.

This leaves only God fearing nations as reasonable options for building this structure. The only God fearing nation in that area during the time period of Moses was the Israelites.

A basic study of the Bible and history would let a person know that the Israelites were not even remotely close to having the type of advanced technoloy that would have been needed during the construction of the Great Pyramid.

The Great Pyramid would not be much of "a

sign and for a witness unto the Lord" if no one from Moses's time period knew why or when it was built. So let's assume that they knew the "when, where, and why" regarding the Great Pyramid.

The natural tendency is to at least try and replicate this awesome structure as your own mini or mid-sized altar to honor the Lord. This is exactly what happened with the Egyptians.

Though I have never seen anything that would indicate that the Egyptians attributed the construction of the Great Pyramid to the Lord, they were in awe of it and therefore, they did try to replicate it.

The best attempts are the two pyramids on either side of the Great Pyramid.

The 2nd largest is the Pyramid of Khafre and the smallest of the three is Pyramid of Menkaure.

I believe that these two pyramids are the "Pillars of Enoch" built using nephilim technologies, but I am not going to go into detail on this as my primary focus point is the Great Pyramid.

Though these two pyramids are impressive at first glance, closer inspection will reveal that they can't compare in any way to the Great Pyramid.

I believe that the Most of the smaller pyramids are rather pathetic when compared to the Great Pyramid. I will give a few photo examples.

By now you are probably wondering where I am going with all this.

My point is that if God wanted an altar built for Him that was intended to be a respectable earthly representation of the heavenly New Jerusalem, He would likely create highly intelligent beings that were specifically wired for these types of task, or in other words "builders", or all of us in the first age.

Acts 4:11 BLB

This is 'the stone having been rejected by you, the builders, which has become the head of the corner.'

To have any ancient people from our current fallen age, where we have fallen flesh bodies and only use around ten percent of our brains, try to build a replica of the heavenly New Jerusalem, would result in the same types of pathetic and dishonorable structures you saw on the previous page.

The Great Pyramid was built in the first earth age before we were under the "law".

Knowing that His people would try and duplicate this altar to Him and that it would end up a disaster and dishonorable, one would think that the Lord would put some type of law or order out that would prevent this from happening.

Believe it or not, this is one of the commands that God gave the Israelites in Exodus chapter twenty.

Exodus 20:25 TLB

You may also build altars from stone, but if you do, then use only uncut stones and boulders. Don't chip or shape the stones with a tool, for that would make them unfit for my altar.

Is this just a coincidence?

It's hard to say for certain. What I can say for certain is that this command was written in the 2D Law or Torah, which makes it highly unlikely that any God-fearing nation existing, during or after the time of Moses, would have built the Great Pyramid even if they had some type of advanced tech that was never recorded.

It is also highly unlikely that any pagan nation would build an altar to the Lord.

In chapter 5, "The Great Pyramid (A Testimony of the First Earth Age)" I demonstrated how it is literally "a sign and for a witness unto the Lord" of the first earth age.

We proved that the "altar to the Lord" mentioned in Isaiah 19:19 is making reference to the Great Pyramid.

 Not only does verse 19 give the exact location of the Great Pyramid, Isaiah 19:19-20 add up (in Hebrew) to the exact inches in height of the pyramid, which is 5,449 inches.

We also have all the other biblical parallels demonstrated in chapter 5, which defy all odds of this being by chance.

I think it's time we take a closer look at Isaiah 19:19-20 and see what we discover.

Isaiah 19:19-20 KJV

19 In that day shall there be an altar to the Lord in the midst of the land of Egypt, and a pillar at the border thereof to the Lord.

20 And it shall be for a sign and for a witness unto the Lord of hosts in the land of Egypt: for they shall cry unto the Lord because of the oppressors, and he shall send them a savior, and a great one and he shall deliver them.

We can see that verse nineteen says,"in that day shall there be an altar to the Lord". This does not give us a specific time period. However, An altar is any structure upon which offerings are made for religious purposes.

Since the Israelites of Moses's time, and after, were commanded not to make altars of cut stone, and the Great Pyramid is made from precisely cut stone, it is also highly unlikely that they would make any offerings to, on, or near, the Great Pyramid.

Therefore we can conclude, with certainty, that the Great Pyramid was built in the very ancient past.

The Great Pyramid existed long before Moses or the Egyptians and the first part of verse twenty clearly says, " And it shall be for a sign and for a witness unto the Lord".

So we have a "sign" and a "witness" from the very ancient past.

This is just further verification of the truth of God's word. The Great Pyramid would not make a very good "witness" if it had not withstood the test of time and it happens to be the only ancient Wonder of the World that still exists today out of the Seven original Wonders of the World.

Though it may have been an altar in the ancient past it is obviously meant to be a witness for all of us that have and currently live on earth.
So now the question is; what is it a "witness" of that pertains to our current earth age?

The answer is that it's a *"witness"* that we came from the previous age, as Job 8:8-9 KJV clearly says and, it is a "witness" in our current age to the fact that we all rejected Jesus as the Headstone and now we exist in fallen flesh bodies, with dead spirits, all within a fallen world, universe, and reality.

It is a *"sign"* that we still have a chance at redemption through Jesus Christ who is the Head of the Church which is represented in the Coming New Jerusalem in which the Great Pyramid was built as an earthly, scaled down, representation, but not an exact copy, of.

The Great Pyramid is not a perfect quadrilateral pyramid (same width, length, and height-) like the New Jerusalem is. It is thought that, at construction, the Great Pyramid was originally 280 Egyptian Royal cubits tall (146.5 metres (480.6 ft)), but with erosion and absence of its pyramidion (capstone), its present height is 138.8 metres (455.4 ft). Each base side was 440 cubits, 230.4 metres (755.9 ft) long.

However, the capstone that represents Jesus, if it existed today, would be a perfect quadrilateral pyramid! It is the same length, width, and height, wich is thirty-feet.

Jesus selflessly came into our fallen world, in a body of flesh, to redeem His bride by taking on our death sentence and paying the price for us.

When He rose again on the third day He was victorious. Death was conquered and He freely offers to bring our spirits back from the dead and give eternal life to all who place their faith in Him and accept His free gift of salvation.

Ephesians 5:14 KJV

Wherefore he saith, Awake thou that sleepest, and arise from the dead, and Christ shall give thee light.

It is not by chance that the Bible clearly says that we are the "builders" that rejected the capstone that represented Jesus Christ as the Head of the Church, and that the Great Pyramid is the only ancient wonder that still exists today.

It has had the capstone missing for all recorded history.

It stands as a *"witness"* to a great rebellion in the first earth age that we took part in.

We would be given a second chance but this earth was now in a fallen state, recreated under the veil of darkness, and we would be sent here as a judgment against us for rejecting the Capstone, but this would also give us the chance to accept Jesus as Savior and be "born again" or redeemed (bought back).

Let's see if we can confirm this in the Bible.

Psalm 82:1 KJV

God standeth in the congregation of the mighty; he judgeth among the gods.

Now let's drop dowm to verses 5-7.

Psalm 82:5-7 KJV

5 They know not, neither will they understand; they walk on in darkness: all the foundations of the earth are out of course.

(This is why our current earth's axis tilts at 23.5 degrees. - Author's note)

6 I have said, Ye are gods; and all of you are children of the most High.

7 But ye shall die like men, and fall like one of the princes.

Verse five verifies what we read in Job 8:8-9 KJV. Psalm 82:5 says *"They know not, neither will they understand; they walk on in darkness"* and Job 8:9 KJV says *"(For we are but of yesterday, and know nothing, because our days upon earth are a shadow:)"*

We must remember that Job 8:8 KJV says " For enquire, I pray thee, of the former age..."

I also want to point out that our current earth age is "the valley of the shadow of death" that David mentions in Psalm 23.

Once we understand this it is clear that God is mocking Job in Job 38 because Job was actually there when God made our current earth age and he doesn't remember or understand. Let's take a look.

Job 38:4-9 KJV

4 Where wast thou when I laid the foundations of the earth? declare, if thou hast understanding. (Remember Psalm 82:5 says "They know not, neither will they understand; they walk on in darkness". Our currently fallen earth age is covered by a veil of darkness- Author's note)

5 Who hath laid the measures thereof, if thou knowest? or who hath stretched the line upon it?

6 Whereupon are the foundations thereof fastened? or who laid the corner stone thereof;

7 When the morning stars sang together, and

all the sons of God shouted for joy?

8 Or who shut up the sea with doors, when it brake forth, as if it had issued out of the womb? (The flood that destroyed the first age - Author's note)

9 When I made the cloud the garment thereof, and thick darkness a swaddlingband for it, (The veil of darkness over our current age - Author's note)

Now if we drop down to verses 26-27 we will see that it mentions *"where no man is"* and *"the desolate and waste ground"* just like we read in Jeremiah 4:25-27 KJV and Isaiah 50:2 KJV.

Job 38:26-27 KJV

26 To cause it to rain on the earth, where no man is; on the wilderness, wherein there is no man;

27 To satisfy the desolate and waste ground; and to cause the bud of the tender herb to spring forth?

If you still doubt that the sons of God sang for joy during the creation of our current, the 2nd earth age, because several people seem to think this happened at the beginning of the first earth age that is mentioned in Genesis 1:1, I will put this to rest now.

Isaiah 14:6 KJV mentions God's judgment against the one He placed in charge (Lucifer) at the end of the first earth age, *"he that ruled the nations"*.

In the very next verse, it mentions God's victory *"the whole earth is at rest"* and then it says *"they break forth in singing"*. This was when He created the foundations for our current age. Let's take a look at this.

Isaiah 14:6-7 KJV

6 He who smote the people in wrath with a continual stroke, he that ruled the nations in anger, is persecuted, and none hindereth.

7 The whole earth is at rest, and is quiet: they break forth into singing.

Remember what we verified earlier in this book, God "quiets The sea" and put the whole earth at rest right after He dashed Rahab into pieces and rebuked Satan.

Job 26:11-13 KJV 1900

"The pillars of heaven are stunned at His rebuke. He quiets The sea with his power, and by his understanding He shatters (maw-khats, dashes asunder), Rahab, by His spirit the heavens were beautiful; His hand forbids the fugitive snake."

We can verify with certainty that this occurred at the end of the first age when Lucifer fell by dropping down to verses 12-14.

Isaiah 14:12-14 KJV

12 How art thou fallen from heaven, O Lucifer, son of the morning! how art thou cut down to the ground, which didst weaken the nations!

13 For thou hast said in thine heart, I will ascend into heaven, I will exalt my throne above the stars of God: I will sit also upon the mount of the congregation, in the sides of the north:

14 I will ascend above the heights of the clouds; I will be like the most High.

Now we have Biblical verification that the morning stars (the angels) sang after Lucifer fell and after the first earth age ended.

These are the morning stars that are mentioned in Job 38:7 when God recreated the earth that we currently live on. The sons of God were there with them. This was you and I when we existed in the former age.

We can take this one step further and be certain that when the Bible mentions the foundations of the earth it is talking about the transition period when God destroyed the former age with water and then began our current age when the angels (the morning stars) sang together and all the sons of God (all of us) shouted for joy because of God's victory over Lucifer.

We find this in Psalm 104 verses 5-6 and Job 38 verse 7.

Psalm 104:5-6 KJV

5 Who laid the foundations of the earth, that it should not be removed for ever.

6 Thou coveredst it with the deep as with a garment: the waters stood above the mountains.

Now we will get Biblical verification that the Bible distinctively separates the angels (the morning stars) from us (the sons of God) during this occurrence.

Job 38:7 KJV

When the morning stars sang together, and all the sons of God shouted for joy?

There are several cases in both the old and new testament where angels and humans are called the sons of God.

However, angels are also often referred to as stars or heavenly host throughout the Bible.

I believe Job 38:7 separates the two by name in this situation to make it clear that two different types of beings were present at this time.

One example of angels referred to as stars in the Bible can be found in Revelation 1:20.

Revelation 1:20 KJV

The mystery of the seven stars which thou sawest in my right hand, and the seven golden candlesticks. The seven stars are the angels of the seven churches: and the seven candlesticks which thou sawest are the seven churches.

At this point God has removed us from earth, *"there was no man"* and we shout for joy at seeing our oppressor Lucifer's defeat and the beginning of a newly restored earth.

However, we have yet to stand trial for our own offense which occurs directly after this and is mentioned in Psalm 82.

Psalm 82:1 KJV

God standeth in the congregation of the mighty; he judgeth among the gods.

So what was God's judgement against us?

Psalm 82: 6-7 KJV

6 I have said, Ye are gods; and all of you are children of the most High.

7 But ye shall die like men, and fall like one of the princes.

I already mentioned that many people think Psalm 82 is referencing angels because they don't realize that there were other beings in the Old Testament (all mankind) that were created to be eternal and also called the sons of God.

They have not solved the great mystery of Christ and the church.

I can understand how an immortal man can be sent here and die as a flesh man. This makes sense because this was OUR sentence.

Psalm 82 is a judgment against us!

Hence, the reason that Jesus took OUR place, and OUR punishment upon Himself, He came as a flesh man (God in the flesh) to die for us.

He took our sentence upon Himself. There is no redemption plan for angels.

Can anyone tell me of one time mentioned in the Bible where a fallen angel takes on flesh and dies?

This would be an angel dying as a man. But the opposite is true when we apply this to angels.

#1. Angels do not die in the flesh (though they can take on the form of flesh) because they are spirits.

#2. God made the Lake of Fire for the devil and His angels.

So it is possible for unsaved man to die like the angels in what the Bible calls the second death, but I don't see anywhere in God's word where angels die like men.

Before we get to the conclusions I would like to point out a fact regarding Genesis that most people skip right past.

I already pointed out that the first earth age was lit by God's glory.

This was before Lucifer rebelled and also before the veil of darkness was placed over our current universe during the recreation.

This means that there weren't any "heavens" in the beginning. There was simply God's glory lighting all creation, or in other words "heaven".

So at the beginning of creation, we would literally just have heaven, singular, and earth.

It was not until after the recreation, during the six days of the creation of our current earth age, that God placed a veil of darkness over our universe due to Lucifer's rebellion.

This veil separated God's glory from creation and formed multiple (three) layers that are referred to as "heavens" in the Bible after this point.

It is not by chance that Genesis 1:1 KJV says "heaven" (singular) and Genesis 2:1, after the six days of recreation, says "heavens" (plural).

Let's take a look.

Genesis 1:1 KJV

In the beginning God created the heaven and the earth.

Genesis 2:1 KJV

Thus the heavens and the earth were finished, and all the host of them.

The following is an excerpt from www.kjvtoday.com

"Heaven" or "Heavens" in Genesis 1:1?

"In the beginning God created the <u>heaven </u>and the earth." **(Genesis 1:1, KJV)**

- Critics charge that שמים (shamayim) is plural and should be translated as "heavens." In Hebrew, however, the plural form may identify size rather than number in certain contexts. Such a plural is called a "plural of extension or amplification" (William Rosenau, *Hebraisms in the Authorized Version of the Bible*, p. 111).

Even in English, the plural form, "skies," is used to refer to a large expanse in the atmosphere which is technically just one sky (e.g. "The plane took to the skies").

Jewish translations of the Tanakh also translate שמים (shamayim) in Genesis 1:1 as "heaven." The *New JPS Translation According to the*

Traditional Hebrew Text says, "heaven."

The 1917 JPS Translation says, "heaven." Moreover, just a few verses later in Genesis 1:8 the NASB and ESV translate שמים as "heaven." The NIV translates it as "sky" (singular). The translators of the NASB, ESV, and NIV all agree that שמים can be translated in the singular. Whether the word should be translated in the singular or plural depends on the translator's assessment of the context.

The KJV translators translated שמים in Genesis 1:1 in the singular because the other heaven (the expanse in the sky) was not created until day two (Genesis 1:7-8). -

If the conclusions in this book are correct, it would mean that Jesus Christ really is the foundation of all reality.

I believe God's word to be true, and it is literal far more often than most people think.

Some people may think that some of the conclusions in this book are just strange chance coincidences that seem to bring quantum physics and the Bible together. This is not by chance. Like I said before, God is the Creator and all true scientific conclusions can and will always confirm God's word.

Jesus truly does come before all things and He represents the quantum level tetrahedron as the foundational building block in our current reality, and the Chief Cornerstone - or Capstone - as the quadrilateral pyramid and building block of an eternal reality. I will point out a few more verses to reaffirm these conclusions.

Job 38:6 mentions God creating our current earth.

Job 38:6 KJV

Whereupon are the foundations thereof fastened? or who laid the corner stone thereof;

If the conclusions you have read in this book are correct, the foundation and Cornerstone would have to be Jesus Christ. Both the Bible and quantum physics confirm this.

1 Corinthians 3:11 HCSB

For no one can lay any other foundation than what has been laid down. That foundation is Jesus Christ.

Psalm 82:6-7 KJV

6 *I have said, Ye are gods; and all of you are children of the most High.*

7 *But ye shall die like men, and fall like one of the princes.*

Romans 3:23-24 ESV

23 *for all have sinned and fall short of the glory of God,*

24 *and are justified by his grace as a gift, through the redemption that is in Christ Jesus*

Isaiah 50:2 KJV

Wherefore, when I came, was there no man? when I called, was there none to answer? Is my hand shortened at all, that it cannot redeem?...

CONCLUSION

We have seen that real science can and does support God's word. In fact, God's word literally forms all creation and reality as we perceive it.

We have seen and verified how this works by God's design in ways never before considered.

We have seen that when the biblical account is brought together with the science of quantum physics and the observable historical data, that the previous earth age can be verified.

Jesus came into our reality, in the flesh, to pay the price for our sins. We are all guilty or we would not be here in this age of death under a death sentence.

Acts 4:11 NLT

For Jesus is the one referred to in the Scriptures, where it says, 'The stone that you builders rejected has now become the cornerstone.

Remember that the Garden of Eden account is a reflection of the eternal order.

In the Garden, Eve was deceived but Adam wasn't. Adam knew fully what he was doing when he ate the fruit. So why did he do it?

I believe Adam stood there looking at the love of his life and knew that Eve was now under a death sentence. I think Adam willingly ate the fruit because he would rather die than be separated from his bride.

This is the same love story we are living right now!

Jesus came to earth because He would rather die than be separated from His bride. The beautiful part is that Jesus could do what Adam never could: conquer death. He accomplished this when He rose from the dead after paying a very steep price to redeem us.

This makes Jesus the Firstborn from this age of death that we are in.

Colossians 1:18 BSB

And He is the head of the body, the church; He is the beginning and firstborn from among the dead, so that in all things He may have preeminence.

Jesus offers you His free gift to all who are willing to accept it.

John 1:12 KJV

But as many as received him, to them gave he power to become the sons of God, even to them that believe on his name:

This is the most important decision you will ever make. Don't put it off, we only get this lifetime to decide - and none of us are guaranteed tomorrow.

2 Corinthians 6:2 KJV

(For he saith, I have heard thee in a time accepted, and in the day of salvation have I succoured thee: behold, now is the accepted time; behold, now is the day of salvation.)

So how can we receive His free gift of salvation?

Romans 10:9-10 KJV

9 *That if thou shalt confess with thy mouth the Lord Jesus, and shalt believe in thine heart that God hath raised him from the dead, thou shalt be saved.*

10 *For with the heart man believeth unto righteousness; and with the mouth confession is made unto salvation.*

AUTHOR'S NOTES

The word of God is His "Whole Message" to mankind. With that in mind, I do not believe there is a single translation that will fully encompass God's word from cover to cover.

I do feel that different translations get the point across better than others, depending on many different variables.

Though I primarily use the King James translation, I feel that other translations are sometimes more easily understood while saying the same thing in many cases.

In *The Gap Fact*, I simply used the translations that I felt would be the easiest to understand in order to explain the different topics we discussed.

I feel the information in this book is critical in order to get a better understanding of God's plan for mankind.

Please help me get this information out. Your good reviews make a big difference and encourage others to take a closer look.

You can leave a review by going to *Amazon.com* and typing in *"the gap fact"*.

Many social media platforms have been violating our freedom of speech and it is getting more difficult for authors like me to share this information. I find myself constantly blocked by the most popular social media sites.

Please tell your friends on Facebook, Twitter, and Google about *The Gap Fact*.

If you enjoyed this book you may be interested in some of my other books that are also available at *Amazon.com*

The Matrix Code and The Alien Agenda

Amazon Reviews:

Donna S.
Five out of Five Stars
"Incredible!"

Gene Hermanski
Five out of Five Stars
"This book will change the way you look at your world!"

The Bible Code Solved

Amazon Reviews:

Christine Fredewricks

Five out of Five Stars
"The Bible Code Solved is inspired by the Holy Spirit in my humble opinion.
"Tracy, you have outdone yourself and grown as an author. I Thank You for allowing yourself to be a willing vessel to allow Yeshua's light to shine thru you to the reader. I now have an ever deeper understanding our our reality, the veil, and the blessed unveiling to come when Jesus returns and soon, I highly recommend this!!!"

Jannell2510
Five out of Five Stars
"New evidence is surfacing that proves God's existence! This book provides that evidence and shows how creation works by God's design."

The Story of Duke

R. Craig
Five out of Five Stars
Amazing, and Outstanding Book! (You may want to grab your tissues before reading!)
"This book is amazing! It grabbed my attention from the first page and held my attention to the last page. I did not want the story to end! What an amazing dog Duke was!

This book is well written, and will leave you wanting more.

I laughed out loud, I cried, and I sat on the edge of my seat in anticipation as to what would happen next. Tracy and Jeanne Yates done an outstanding job on this book! I give this book 5 stars and hope to see more books by one or both of these authors!"

Christy
Five out of Five Stars
"Kleenex is needed -

This was an amazing book. It made me cry and laugh (out loud) I fell in love with Duke and found myself praying right along with Matt. Make sure you have some Kleenex when you read this one."

Made in the USA
Middletown, DE
07 October 2023

40381084R00203